Nonsexist Research Methods

Nonsexist Research Methods

A Practical Guide

MARGRIT EICHLER
Ontario Institute for Studies in Education

ROUTLEDGE
New York   London

7|8|10

Published in 1988 by Allen and Unwin, Inc.
Reprinted in 1991 by
Routledge
An imprint of Routledge, Chapman and Hall, Inc.
29 West 35 Street
New York, NY 10001

Published in Great Britain by

Routledge
11 New Fetter Lane
London EC4P 4EE

Library of Congress Cataloging-in-Publication Data

Eichler, Margrit.
    Nonsexist research methods.
    Bibliography: p.
    Includes index.
    1. Social sciences — Research.   2. Sexism.   I. Title.
H62.E453   1987   300'.72   87-11477
ISBN 0-04-497044-7
ISBN 0-415-90605-9 (pb)

British Library Catalouging in Publication Data

Eichler, Margrit
    Nonsexist research methods: a practical guide.
    1. Sexism in social science research
    I. Title.
    300'.72   H62
    ISBN 0-04-497044-7
    ISBN 0-415-90605-9

Contents

Acknowledgments

This book is the result of several years of study in the area of sexism in scholarship and nonsexist alternatives. It has thus profited immensely from the various debates and publications on this topic. Many but not all of the authors who have contributed to this debate are cited in the text. I have also profited over the years from discussions with students. In particular, however, I am grateful to Paula Caplan, Marjorie Cohen, Jill Vickers, Marylee Stephenson, and Wendy McKeen for reading and commenting on the entire manuscript, and to Robert Brym and Rhonda Lenton for reading and commenting on portions of the manuscript. The comments of the readers also resulted in several important changes in the final version. Finally, my greatest debt goes to Linda Williams, who provided invaluable research assistance at various points during the writing of the book.

I would also like to thank the following people for providing me with specific references: Paula Caplan, Ursula Franklin, Ester Greenglass, Thelma McCormack, Paul Olson, Ruth Pierson, Monica Townson, and Paul Wiesenthal.

The guidelines contained in the book have gone through many revisions and applications. Part of them were developed within the framework of a federal committee, the Canadian Women's Studies

Advisory Committee of the Secretary of State's Women's Programme. This committee was established to advise the federal government on where to locate five chairs on women's studies endowed by the Canadian government for the five geographic regions of Canada. Having received a broad rather than narrow mandate, the committee added the development of a set of guidelines for nonsexist research to its agenda. The entire committee, consisting of June Gow (chair), Donna Greschner, Gilberte Leblanc, Donna Mergler, Beth Percival, Charlotte Thibault, Jennifer Stoddart, and myself screened and discussed two earlier versions of the guidelines contained in this book. In particular, Donna Mergler contributed to the present shape of the guidelines.

Finally, I wish to acknowledge gratefully the excellent copy-editing done by Patricia Miller. Lisa Freeman-Miller of Allen & Unwin was a dream come true in what you hope for in an editor.

Chapter 1
Sexism in Research

1.1 Introduction

Over a century ago, a schoolmaster named Edwin A. Abbott wrote an amusing "Romance of Many Dimensions," entitled *Flatland*,[1] in which he described the adventures of the Square, a being from a two-dimensional universe (Flatland), who explores a one-dimensional universe (Lineland) and a three-dimensional universe (Spaceland).

1

The Square describes the inability of the King of Lineland, a one-dimensional being, to grasp the essence of a two-dimensional universe, and then describes his own incapacity to believe in the existence of a three-dimensional universe. It is only when he is physically lifted out of his own universe and sees it from above (a dimension that is nonexistent in his own Flatland) that he becomes capable of intellectually grasping the existence of three-dimensional space.

When the Square returns to his own country, he eagerly tries to spread the Gospel of Three Dimensions, but is predictably put into prison as a dangerous lunatic, where he languishes at the end of the novel, "absolutely destitute of converts."

The following is an excerpt in which our hero, the Square, tries to convince the King of Lineland that there are, in fact, two dimensions. He argues that, in addition to Lineland's motions of Northward and Southward, which are the only directions in which lines can move in Lineland, there is another motion, which he calls from right to left:

KING: *Exhibit to me, if you please, this motion from left to right.*
I: *Nay, that I cannot do, unless you could step out of your Line altogether.*
KING: *Out of my Line? Do you mean out of the world? Out of Space?*
I: *Well, yes. Out of your Space. For your Space is not the true Space. True Space is a Plane; but your Space is only a Line.*
KING: *If you cannot indicate this motion from left to right by yourself moving in it, then I beg you to describe it to me in words.*
I: *If I cannot tell your right side from your left, I fear that no words of mine can make my meaning clear to you. But surely you cannot be ignorant of so simple a distinction.*
KING: *I do not in the least understand you.* (Abbott, 1952:62)

Like the King of Lineland, we have been brought up in an intellectually limited universe. Our dilemma is that all our major concepts, our way of seeing reality, our willingness to accept proof, have been shaped by one dimension – one sex – rather than by two. For as long as we remain within this intellectual universe, we are incapable of comprehending its limitations, believing it to be the only world that exists. In order to truly understand our universe, we must create a vantage point that allows us to observe it both for what it is and for what it is not. Not an easy task, as the Square found out when he tried to explain the existence of left and right to a person who had never experienced them.

Similarly, none of us has ever lived in a nonsexist society: moving toward nonsexist scholarship is comparable to trying to comprehend a dimension that we have not materially experienced. We can describe it in theoretical terms, but we cannot fully appreciate its nature until we are able to lift ourselves out of our current confining parameters. This involves becoming aware of sexism in research and starting to eliminate it.

Sexism in research was first recognized as a major problem around the mid-1970s. While books and articles that pointed out the problem existed before that time,[2] it is only since the mid-1970s that critiques have appeared with some regularity and in more mainstream outlets.

In the early 1970s and continuing into the 1980s, various organizations, publishers, and publication outlets began adopting rules about the use of nonsexist language,[3] and recently, about nonsexist content.[4] Nevertheless, sexism in research is still badly understood. Even less well understood is how to conduct research in a nonsexist manner.

This book has two major objectives: (1) to present an analysis of sexism in research that enlarges our understanding of this problem and sensitizes students and researchers to sexism in its various manifestations; and (2) to provide guidelines for solving the problem that offer clear and concise means of creating nonsexist alternatives.

1.2 Sexism in Research

Most analyses of sexism in research focus either on one discipline or subject area or else on one type of sexism.[5] Indeed, we do not tend to speak of "types of sexism," but of "sexism," pure and simple.[6] The term "sexism" suggests that we are dealing with *one* problem that may manifest itself in different areas differently, but which nevertheless is a single basic problem – what one might call the "big blob" theory of sexism.

This book takes a different approach. Sexism is here broken down into seven different types. Of these seven types, four are primary and three are derived. *Primary problems* are those that cannot be reduced one to the other, although they coexist and often overlap. *Derived problems* are problems that are not logically distinct from the primary problems but which appear so frequently that they warrant being identified by a special label. The primary problems are: (1) *androcentricity*, (2) *overgeneralization*, (3) *gender insensitivity*, and (4) *double standards*. Derived problems are: (5) *sex appropriateness*, (6) *familism*, and (7) *sexual dichotomism*. There is a certain arbitrariness about identifying seven, rather than, say, six or five or eight sexist problems in research.[7] There is also a certain arbitrariness in the manner in which the boundaries have been drawn. The seven problems presented here have emerged through many attempts to order the otherwise diverse materials concerning critiques of sexism. The success of the approach presented here does not depend on acceptance of this categorization as the best possible or on correctly pigeonholing empirical problems under their appropriate theoretical labels, however. Instead, what is important is recognizing that sexism is multidimensional rather than unidimensional, identifying a sexist problem as such, and rectifying it. In other words, the seven problems are intended to serve as tools to facilitate the recognition and correction of sexism in research, rather than as an ultimate system of categorization.

It is helpful to think of the four primary problems as a set of movable circles. They all have a different core, and sometimes they overlap very heavily, sometimes only at the periphery, sometimes not at all. Occasionally, all four circles may overlap. Thus there may be more than one correct classification of a problem. The three derived problems, in contrast, can be thought of as constituting inner rings that are strongly defined within two of those larger circles.

The following preliminary definitions of all seven problems will be expanded in Chapters 2–6, where more extensive illustrations are provided. Chapter 7, organized by components of the research process, offers a set of guidelines for detecting and eliminating sexism in research.

1.3 The Seven Sexist Problems

1.3.1 Androcentricity

Androcentricity is essentially a view of the world from a male perspective. It manifests itself when ego is constructed as male rather than female, such as when "intergroup warfare" is defined as a "means of gaining women and slaves." In this case, the "group" is defined as consisting only of males, since the women are what is "gained." From an androcentric perspective, women are seen as passive objects rather than subjects in history, as acted upon rather than actors; androcentricity prevents us from understanding that both males and females are always acted upon as well as acting, although often in very different ways. Two extreme forms of androcentricity are *gynopia* (female invisibility) and *misogyny* (hatred of women).

This definition raises a difficulty that must be acknowledged. Theoretically speaking, problems of perspective could come in two versions: one female, one male. The female version would be gynocentricity, or a view of the world from a female perspective. I have labeled this problem androcentricity rather than, for instance, andro-gynocentricity for two reasons. First, the problem is so overwhelmingly biased in the male direction that to accord a female version of the problem equal status would be inappropriate. I have, however, included the few examples of incipient gynocentricity that I found in my search of the literature. Second, it is not really possible to find a form of gynocentricity that is in any way comparable to androcentricity, for the simple reason that we live in an androcentric social, political, and intellectual environment. Thus even when we attempt to take a *consciously* female perspective, this attempt occurs within an overall intellectual environment in which both our vehicle for thought (language) and the content of thought (concepts) are colored by thousands of years of overwhelmingly androcentric thinking. It is therefore both misleading and inaccurate to treat possible gynocentricity as comparable to actual androcentricity. However, it is important to acknowledge that sexism can theoretically come in two forms, and to remind ourselves that neither is acceptable in scholarship.

1.3.2 Overgeneralization/Overspecificity

Overgeneralization occurs when a study deals with only one sex but presents itself as if it were applicable to both sexes. Its flip side is overspecificity, which occurs when a study is reported in such a manner that it is impossible to determine whether or not it applies to one or both sexes. Using a sample of male workers and calling it a study of social class is an instance of overgeneralization; the same problem arises when one uses the term "parents" to refer exclusively to mothers (ignoring fathers). Overspecificity occurs when single-sex terms are used when members of both sexes are involved (e.g., "the doctor . . . he, or "man is a mammal"). Many (but not all) of the problems involving sexist language belong in this category.

There is considerable overlap between overgeneralization/overspecificity and androcentricity. Nevertheless, one cannot be equated to the other. A study may be androcentric without being overgeneral, such as when male violence against women is dismissed as trivial or unimportant (thus maintaining male over female interests) although the actors are correctly identified by their sex. A study may also be overgeneral or overspecific without being necessarily androcentric, such as when a study uses all male subjects (e.g., male students) or all female subjects (e.g., mothers) but presents the findings in general terms ("students" respond well to ability grouping, or "parents" tend to teach their children concepts through ostensive definitions).

1.3.3 Gender Insensitivity

Gender insensitivity is a simple problem: it consists of ignoring sex as a socially important variable. It sometimes overlaps with overgeneralization/overspecificity, but the two are not identical: In the case of general insensitivity, sex is ignored to such a degree that the presence of overgeneralization or androcentricity cannot even be identified. If a study simply fails to report the sex of its respondents, or if a policy study completely ignores the different effects of, let us say, a particular unemployment insurance policy on the two sexes, then we cannot identify whether male or female subjects were included or whether males or females would differentially profit from or be hurt by a particular policy. In a completely gender-insensitive study, it would be impossible to identify other problems because information necessary to do so is missing.

1.3.4 Double Standards

The use of double standards involves evaluating, treating, or measuring identical behaviors, traits, or situations by different means. A double standard is by no means easy to identify, although it may sound easy: it involves recognizing behaviors, traits, or situations as identical when they bear different labels or are described in different terms. For instance, some psychological disorders occur only in one sex. To find out whether or not a given example is an instance of the application of a double standard, one must (1) identify a larger category for the disorder; (2) determine whether there is a complementary disorder for the other sex; (3) identify whether the two are equivalent; and (4) determine whether they are evaluated in different ways. Only when all these preconditions obtain are we dealing with a double standard. If the disorder appears in only one sex, no double standard is involved.

Identification is not made easier by the fact that a researcher may have used different instruments to measure identical attributes of the sexes. For example, social status is currently derived by using different measures for the sexes (for further discussion of this specific problem, see Chapter 5). However, this different measurement coincides with an actual difference in social standing between the sexes, a difference that we are incapable of measuring adequately because we have no sex-free instrument at our disposal. Identification of a double standard thus involves distancing oneself to some degree from the social context as it is presented – not a simple thing to do, and never perfectly achieved.

A double standard is likely to be inspired by, or lead to, androcentricity, but it need not necessarily do so. Using female-derived categories of social status for women and male-derived categories for men is an instance of a double standard in the use of instruments, but it is neither gender insensitive nor androcentric nor overgeneral/overspecific.

1.3.5 Sex Appropriateness

Sex appropriateness, our first "derived" category, is nothing but a particular instance of a double standard, one that is so accepted within the relevant literature that it is proudly acknowledged with special terms: for example, "appropriate sex roles," or "appropriate gender identity." The absence of appropriate gender identity is called *dysphoria*, and it is classed as a psychological disorder. Sex appropriateness becomes a problem when *human* traits or attributes are assigned only to one sex or the other and are treated as more important for the sex to which they have been assigned. It is *not* a problem when we are dealing with a truly sex-specific attribute, such as the capacity to ejaculate or to give birth to children. It *is* a problem when it is applied to such human capacities as child rearing (as opposed to child bearing).

This particular example of a double standard has been singled out from the overall discussion of double standards because sex appropriateness is still widely accepted within the social science literature as a legitimate concept.

1.3.6 Familism

Familism is a particular instance of gender insensitivity. It consists of treating the family as the smallest unit of analysis in instances in which it is, in fact, individuals within families (or households) who engage in certain actions, have certain experiences, and so on. It is *not* a problem of sexism when no such attribution occurs. Another manifestation of familism occurs when the family is assumed to be uniformly affected (positively or negatively) in instances in which the same event may have different effects on various family members.

This problem has been singled out from the general discussion of gender insensitivity for the same reason that sex appropriateness has been singled out from the discussion of double standards: It is a very well-accepted practice within the social sciences to engage in familism, and is, at present, still considered to be entirely legitimate.

1.3.7 Sexual Dichotomism

Sexual dichotomism is another subaspect of the use of double standards. It involves the treatment of the sexes as two entirely discrete social, as well as biological, groups, rather than as two groups with overlapping characteristics. It leads to an exaggeration of sex differences of all types at the expense of recognizing *both* the differences *and* the similarities between the sexes. It is particularly important to recognize sexual dichotomism as a form of sexism because it is sometimes used as a "cure" for gender insensitivity. When this occurs, it is simply a case of substituting one form of sexism for another; and it is doubly misleading because it creates the illusion of having achieved a solution.

1.4 Organization and History of this Book

This book is organized around two major axes: type of sexist problem, and component of the research process in which particular types of problems may appear. Chapters 2 through 5 each deal with one primary problem, Chapter 6 deals with the three derived problems, and Chapter 7 and the checklist (see Appendix) are organized around the various components of the research process. This structure evolved after a period of trial and error in which I tried to organize the book only around the type of problem, or only around the research components. Being dissatisfied with both, I eventually settled on a compromise structure that combines both organizing principles.

The problem-oriented chapters include examples drawn from actual research. The majority are taken from recent issues of journals, mostly from 1985. Occasionally, other publications are used (books, reports of committees), and occasionally I also draw on other researchers' critiques of sexism. However, the ease with which examples can be drawn from academic journals demonstrates the pervasiveness of sexism: It exists in every social science discipline[8] and in virtually any nonfeminist publication, no matter how respectable or how current. Moreover, the problems are similar regardless of discipline or publication outlet.[9]

My method was simple: I went into a library and picked up whatever recent issue of journals from different disciplines was lying on top in the journal pigeon holes. I assumed that it would make little difference which journal or issue I picked, and that I would find at least one example of sexism in every single one.[10] Sadly, this turned out to be correct.

This method of finding many of my examples also points to a major limitation in this book that must be made clear: There is a large element of chance involved in who and what gets cited. Depending on which journal issue I picked up first, the example may have been taken from psychology when I could just as well have taken it from anthropology or sociology. The same applies to authors. The examples presented here are, therefore, just that: examples, no more, no less. They are not indicative of the degree or type of sexism prevalent in any particular author, field of investigation, or discipline.

It is possible, indeed likely, that particular problems are more prevalent in certain disciplines or subject areas than in others (or indeed, that a particular problem does *not* occur in some disciplines). However, to demonstrate this is not a task undertaken in this book. It is clearly a second step. Nor is there any intent to pronounce on the relative frequency or importance of each of the problems. That, too, is clearly a second step. The intention here is simply to demonstrate the existence of distinct types of sexism that occur in the social sciences, to offer means for their identification, and to provide suggestions for their solution.

Chapter 7 presents a systematic discussion of potential sexist problems following the various components of the research process. Because the analysis is meant to be generally applicable to various disciplines and methodological approaches, not all components are applicable to all studies. For instance, many studies do not have a policy component. Other studies do not ask direct questions of respondents. All studies, on the other hand, presumably use major concepts, have a title, and ask a research question, even if only implicitly. In addition, please note that although the guidelines have gone through a process of considerable testing and revision, I make no claim that all the problems of sexism in research are included in them. We are constantly becoming aware of new problems.

The guidelines set forth in Chapter 7 are meant to assist in the identification and eventual resolution of sexist problems. They do not, of course, solve other research problems: a study may be entirely nonsexist and still be trivial or otherwise bad research. However, a study cannot be sexist and constitute good research. The guidelines therefore spell out a set of necessary but not sufficient criteria for good research.

1.5 Sexism and Scientific Objectivity

One spinoff from the various critiques of sexism in research has been a renewed doubt about the possibility of objectivity in the social sciences. While academicians have traditionally assumed that objectivity is a hallmark of their work, feminist scholars have challenged this assumption. Some feminist researchers even maintain that objectivity is, in principle, impossible to achieve, and that the most we can do is to admit to an unabashed subjectivity, our own as well as everybody else's.[11] However, the logical consequence of such a principled stance is that research, including the implied cumulative knowledge it generates, is impossible.

This seems rather like throwing out the baby with the bathwater. Instead, it is more useful to identify the various components commonly included under the heading of objectivity and look at them separately, in order to eliminate the problematic aspects of objectivity while maintaining the useful ones. One scholar who engages in such a process of separating useful from harmful components of objectivity is Elizabeth Fee.[12] She suggests that the following "aspects of scientific objectivity . . . should be preserved and defended":

> The concept of creating knowledge through a constant process of practical interaction with nature, the willingness to consider all assumptions and methods as open to question and the expectation that ideas will be subjected to the most unfettered critical evaluation. . . .[13]

Fee also rejects certain aspects of "objectivity" in research. For example, she rejects as not helpful the notion that objectivity requires a distancing of the researcher from the subject matter, and of the production of knowledge from its uses. Likewise, she rejects as unnecessary the divorce between scientific rationality and emotional or social commitment; she also rejects the assumption that knowledge must flow only from the expert to the nonexpert and thus that a dialogue is not possible. She deplores the prevailing split between subject and object, in which the knowing mind is active and the object of knowledge entirely passive. Such a structure of knowledge results in a depersonalized voice of abstract authority that legitimizes domination. Finally, she rejects as impossible the complete freedom of research from its sociopolitical environment.

Though she focuses on the concept of the "scientific process" and not on "objectivity" per se, Karen Messing argues that "the ideology and the background of the researcher" can influence the research process at eleven different stages:[14]

- the selection of the scientists,
- their access to facilities for scientific work,
- the choice of research topic,
- the wording of the hypothesis,
- the choice of experimental subjects,
- the choice of appropriate controls,
- the method of observation,
- data analysis,
- interpretation of data,
- the publication of results,
- and the popularization of results.[15]

Jill McCalla Vickers list as one of her methodological rebellions "the rebellion against objectivity,"[16] which she sees as (a) "treating those you study as objects and objectifying their pains in words which hide the identity of their oppressors," or (b) "being detached from that which is studied."[17] She accepts objectivity as "the rules which are designed to facilitate intersubjective transmissibility, testing, replication, etc."[18]

Finally, Evelyn Fox Keller has beautifully demonstrated that objectivity has been largely equated with masculinity.[19] She discusses particularly the misconception that objectivity requires detachment of the knower, both in emotional as well as in intellectual terms. Moreover, she argues that

> the disengagement of our thinking about science from our notions of what is masculine could lead to a freeing of both from some of the rigidities to which they have been bound, with profound ramifications for both. Not only, for example, might science become more accessible to women, but, far more importantly, our very conception of "objective" could be freed from inappropriate constraints. As we begin to understand the ways in which science itself has been influenced by its unconscious mythology, we can begin to perceive the possibilities for a science not bound by such mythology.[20]

It seems, then, that it is possible to be critical of the way in which objectivity has been defined without having to abandon the concept and sink into the morass of complete cultural subjectivism. We need to separate clearly objectivity from detachment and from the myth that research is value-free. Neither of the latter two conditions is, in principle, possible for any researcher (or anybody else). Our values will always intrude in a number of ways into the research process, beginning with the choice of the research question; and we will necessarily always be informed by a particular perspective. Nor is there any need to detach ourselves emotionally from the research process – in fact, this is impossible, and what appears as scholarly detachment is in reality only a matter of careful disguise.

Objectivity remains a useful and important goal for research in the following ways:

(1) a commitment to look at contrary evidence;

(2) a determination to aim at maximum replicability of any study (which implies accurate reporting of all processes employed and separation between simple reporting and interpretation, to the degree that these are possible);

(3) a commitment to "truth-finding" (what Kenneth Boulding has called veracity);[21] and

(4) a clarification and classification of values underlying the research: nonsexist research, for instance, is, based on the value judgment that the sexes are of equal worth, while androcentric research grows out of the belief that men are of higher worth (and therefore more important) than women.

I find it useful to think of objectivity as an asymptotically approachable but unreachable goal, with the elimination of sexism in research as a station along the way.

1.6 Solving the Problem of Sexism in Research

When we regard a problem as simple, a single solution often seems appropriate. Once we begin to differentiate among different and distinct components of a problem, however, different and distinct solutions become a necessity. When we fail to make the proper distinctions, we may – unwittingly and despite the very best intentions – replace one problem of sexism with another.

The analysis of sexism in language provides a case in point. Early and incisive studies of sexism in language convinced a number of organizations and individuals that sexist language was unacceptable in scholarly research (or elsewhere, for that matter!).[22] Typically, these analyses pointed out the use of so-called generic male terms as sexist, and often they included reference to such demeaning terms as "girls" for "women," or nonparallel terms (Mrs. John Smith but not Mr. Anne Smith, or the use of Mrs. or Miss, which indicate marital status, versus Mr., which does not).

As a consequence of these critiques, guides were published that replaced so-called generic male terms with truly generic terms: policeman became police officer; fireman, fire fighter; postman, mail carrier; workman, worker; chairman, chairperson; mankind, humanity; and so on. In effect, occupational and other terms were "desexed." The generic "he" was replaced with "he or she," or "s/he," or "they," or "one," or "people," and so on. Guides of this type continue to be important and useful, but unless care is taken as to how and when and in what context these gender-neutral terms are used, another form of sexism may inadvertently enter the picture.

The use of male (or sex-specific) terms for generic situations is one form of overgeneralization, one of our sexist problems. However, there is another aspect to the same problem: the use of generic terms for sex-specific situations, which is just as problematic as is the first manifestation. For example, if researchers talk about workers in general while only having studied male workers (constantly and cautiously using "they," "people," "the individual," "the person," and so on, with nary a female in sight), they simply replace one sexist problem with another in the manner in which language is used.[23] Language that employs "nonsexist" generic terms for sex-specific situations creates the same problem in reverse and constitutes at one and the same time an example of both overgeneralization and gender insensitivity.[24] In other words, when the content is sex specific, the language used should also be sex specific.

Sexism takes more than one form, and therefore ways to combat it may also take more than one form. The trick is to develop criteria that help us determine which solution is appropriate when. This is the major purpose of this book.

Notes

1　Edwin A. Abbott, *Flatland: A Romance of Many Dimensions* (New York: Dover, 1952).

2　See, for instance, Ruth Hershberger, *Adam's Rib* (New York: Harper & Row, 1970), first published in 1948; or the special issue on sexism in family studies of the *Journal of Marriage and the Family* 33: 3, 4 (1971).

3　An early example are the guidelines by Scott, Foresman and Co., "Guidelines for improving the image of women in textbooks" (Glenview, IL, 1972); see also "Guidelines for equal treatment of the sexes in McGraw-Hill Book Company publications" (n.d.); "Guidelines for nonsexist use of language," prepared by the American Psychological Association Task Force on Issues of Sexual Bias in Graduate Education, *American Psychologist* (June 1975): 682–684; "Guidelines for nonsexist use of language in National Council of Teachers of English publications" (March 1976).

4　For example, the Canadian Psychological Association approved a set of nonsexist guidelines in 1983; see Cannie Stark-Adamec and Meredith Kimball, "Science free of sexism: A psychologist's guide to the conduct of nonsexist research," *Canadian Psychology* 25: 1 (1984): 23–34. The Canadian Sociology and Anthropology Association passed a motion at its general annual meeting in 1984 that all official publications must be nonsexist in language and content; see Margrit Eichler, "And the work never ends: Feminist contributions," *Canadian Review of Sociology and Anthropology* 22, 5 (1985): 619–644, esp. p. 633; "AERA guidelines for eliminating race and sex bias in educational research and evaluation," *Educational Researcher* 14, 6 (1985). The American Sociological Association published a set of guidelines in one of its publications; see "Sexist biases in sociological research: Problems and issues," *ASA Footnotes* (January 1980): 8–9, but its major journal, the *American Sociological Review*, does not require that articles be nonsexist in language and content. The Social Sciences and Humanities Research Council in Canada published a booklet suggesting that sexist research is bad research; see Margrit Eichler and Jeanne Lapointe, "On the treatment of the sexes in research" (Ottawa: Social Sciences and Humanities Research Council of Canada, Minister of Supply and Services, 1985); however, the assessment forms for projects do not include a criterion that the research be nonsexist. For an overview of strategies adopted by Canadian professional social science organizations and scholarly journals, see Linda Christiansen-Ruffman et al., "Sex bias in research: Current awareness and strategies to eliminate bias within Canadian social science" (Report of the Task Force on the Elimination of Sexist Bias in Research to the Social Science Federation of Canada, 1986).

5 See, for instance, Shulamit Reinharz, Marti Bombyk, and Janet Wright, "Method-ological issues in feminist research: A bibliography of literature in women's studies, sociology and psychology," *Women's Studies International Forum* 6, 4 (1983): 437–454; and Margrit Eichler with the assistance of Rhonda Lenton, Somer Brodribb, Jane Haddad, and Becki Ross, "A selected annotated bibliography on sexism in research" (Ottawa: Social Sciences and Humanities Research Council of Canada, 1985).

6 This is not always true. Sexism is occasionally broken down into different ways in which it manifests itself, but such different manifestations are usually *not* seen as logically distinct. As an example, see Kathryn B. Ward and Linda Grant, "The feminist critique and a decade of published research in sociology journals," *Sociological Quarterly* 26, 2 (1985): 139–157.

7 Indeed, my first attempt to identify a set of superordinate sexist problems involved six, rather than seven problems; see Margrit Eichler, "Les six péchés capitaux sexistes," in Huguette Dagenais (ed.) *Approches et methodes de la recherche féministe*. Actes du colloque organisé par le Groupe de recherche multidisciplinaire féministe, Mai 1985. (Université Laval: Maquettiste, 1968): 17–29.

8 I do not mean to imply that the problem does not exist in the natural sciences as well. Indeed, we know that it does, as recent analyses have eloquently demonstrated; see, for example, Ruth Hubbard, Mary Sue Henifin, and Barbara Fried (eds.), *Women Look at Biology Looking at Women: A Collection of Feminist Critiques* (Cambridge, MA: Schenkman, 1979); Ruth Bleier, *Science and Gender: A Critique of Biology and Its Theories on Women* (New York: Pergamon Press, 1984); Marian Lowe and Ruth Hubbard (eds.), *Woman's Nature: Rationalizations of Inequality* (New York: Pergamon, 1983); Sandra Harding and Merrill B. Hintikka

(eds.), *Discovering Reality: Feminist Perspectives on Epistemology, Metaphysics, Methodology, and Philosophy of Science* (Dordrecht: D. Reidel, 1983). This book restricts itself to the social sciences for the simple reason that I am not competent to write about the natural sciences.

9 Feminist writings may be sexist as well. However, since the likelihood is much smaller than with nonfeminist writings, my search would have been much more arduous, and it simply is not the major problem, I did not include feminist journals in my search.

10 However, it should be noted that I did apply a criterion in selecting journals from within the same discipline: In cases where there were several journals from the same discipline, I favored the ones with the longest run, as indicated by volume number (the higher the number, the longer the run) on the assumption that the older the journal, the more established it could be assumed to be. In addition, the selection is heavily biased toward U.S. and Canadian journals.

11 This is, for instance, the position taken by Liz Stanley and Sue Wise in *Breaking Out: Feminist Consciousness and Feminist Research* (London: Routledge & Kegan Paul, 1983). They argue

> We don't believe that "science" exists in the way that many people still claim it does. We don't see it as the single-minded objective pursuit of truth. "Truth" is a social construct, in the same way that "objectivity" is; and both are constructed out of experiences which are, for all practical purposes, the same as "lies" and "subjectivity." And so we sell all research as "fiction" in the sense that it views and so constructs "reality" through the eyes of one person. (p. 174)

12 Elizabeth Fee, "Women's nature and scientific objectivity," in Marian Lowe and Ruth Hubbard (eds.), *Women's Nature: Rationalizations of Inequality* (New York: Pergamon, 1983): 9–27.

13 Ibid., p. 16.

14 Karen Messing, "The scientific mystique: Can a white lab coat guarantee purity in the search for knowledge about the nature of women?" in Marian Lowe and Ruth Hubbard (eds.), *Women's Nature: Rationalizations of Inequality* (New York: Pergamon, 1983):75–88.

15 Ibid., p. 76.

16 Jill McCalla Vickers, "Memoirs of an ontological exile: The methodological rebellions of feminist research," in Angela Miles and Geraldine Finn (eds.), *Feminism in Canada: From Pressure to Politics* (Montreal: Black Rose, 1982): 27–46.

17 Ibid., p. 40.

18 Ibid. In a more recent article, Vickers pushes toward a new epistemology; see Jill Vickers, "So then what? Issues in feminist epistemology." Unpublished paper presented at the 4th annual meeting of the Canadian Women's Studies Association,Winnipeg,1986.

19 Evelyn Fox Keller, *Reflections on Gender and Science* (New Haven: Yale University Press, 1985).

20 Ibid., pp. 92–93.

21 Kenneth E. Boulding, "Learning by simplifying complexity: How to turn data into

knowledge," in *The Science and Praxis of Complexity*, contributions to the symposium held at Montpellier, France, 1984 (Tokyo: United Nations University, 1985): 31. I would like to thank Ursula Franklin for drawing my attention to this quote.

22 Some of the early studies include Virginia Kidd, "A study of images produced through the use of a male pronoun as the generic," *Movements: Contemporary Rhetoric and Communication* (Fall 1971): 25–30; Joseph W. Schneider and Sally L. Hacker, "Sex role imagery and the use of generic man in introductory texts," *American Sociologist* 8 (1973): 12–18; some of the later studies include Jeannette Silveira, "Generic masculine words and thinking," *Women's Studies International Quarterly* 3, 2/3 (1980): 165–178; Janice Moulton, George M. Robinson, and Cherin Elias, "Sex bias in language use: "Neutral" pronouns that aren't," *American Psychologist* 33, 11 (1978): 1032–1036; Mary Vetterling-Braggin (ed.), *Sexist Language: A Modern Philosophical Analysis* (Totowa, NJ: Littlefield, Adams, 1981); John Briere and Cheryl Lanktree, "Sex-role related effects of sex bias in language," *Sex Roles* 9, 5 (1983): 625–632.

23 There is one exception to this general rule. When a communication is intended to solicit the representation of both sexes, even though only one is represented at a given point in time, it may be appropriate to use nonsexist language, as in announcements advertising jobs so far held only by men (for example, fire fighters, police officers, or chairpersons).

24 Another instance in which an attempt to avoid sexism may inadvertently lead to another type of sexism occurs when researchers trying to avoid gender insensitivity fall into the error of sexual dichotomism by treating sex as a categorical variable for all sorts of social phenomena.

Chapter 2
Androcentricity

2.1 Introduction

Androcentricity is, in its most basic expression, a vision of the world in male terms, a reconstruction of the social universe from a male perspective. Specifically, it expresses itself in a construction of ego as male rather than female, with a concomitant view of females as objects rather than subjects, as acted upon rather than as actors. The male is the reference point; the female, the "other," is located in relation to him, as Simone de Beauvoir has so eloquently argued.[1]

Androcentricity results in the maintenance of male over female interests. This may take the form of trivializing problems experienced by women, where males are the originators of these problems, or it can take the form of an argument for maintaining a situation that favors males over females. Further, it can lead to a failure of vision, what Shulamit Reinharz has called *gynopia*: "the inability to perceive the very existence of women as fully human actors."[2] The extreme form of androcentricity is outright misogyny: hatred of women.

Theoretically, sexism in research could take the form of either androcentricity or gynocentricity (in which the world is perceived in female terms, the social universe is reconstructed from a female perspective, and so on). Realistically speaking, however, the problem is not gynocentricity but androcentricity, quite simply because men constitute the dominant sex, not women. Occasionally we find examples of incipient gynocentricity, but they are rare indeed. Finally, androcentricity may be practiced by both male and female authors. Being born female does not make one automatically capable of transcending androcentricity. Likewise, being born male does not prevent one from conducting nonsexist research and writing in a nonsexist manner.

In this chapter, we will first consider various ways in which androcentricity manifests itself. This is followed by a discussion of the stages of the research process in which it may appear.

2.2 Types of Androcentricity

2.2.1 Male Viewpoint or Frame of Reference

A male viewpoint or frame of reference results in the construction of the actor as male rather than as either male or female or both female and male, while at the same time asserting general applicability. It leads to female invisibility, helps to maintain male over female interests, and may lead to blaming women. It is thus a shorthand expression for a conglomerate of aspects of androcentricity that will be dealt with in the following sections. In addition, however, it indicates a commitment to an androcentric theory, framework, model of reality, or way of proceeding, even when the sexism has become obvious. We will consider just one example of this here.

In a passage on social ascription and social theory, the author discusses racial-ethnic and gender ascription in the human capital and structural functionalist literatures. He notes that

> while it is difficult to summarize and analyse them briefly and neatly, they all orbit around some conception of efficiency, both narrowly economic and otherwise. Thus, when the economic returns to human capital are found to be less for some racial-ethnic groups than for others, or less for women than for men, it is often assumed (rather than shown) that this occurs because of some unmeasured sources of racial-ethnic or gender differences in productivity. . . . The reason for this is most likely that, according to the principles of marginal productivity theory, the distribution of marginal products *is* identical with the distribu[t]ion of earned income. . . . And one naturally hesitates to remove one of the cornerstones from the edifice of modern microeconomics on grounds of a few tenants who apparently cannot be accommodated.[3]

After a fair criticism of sexism in microeconomics, the author suggests that one "naturally hesitates to remove one of the cornerstones . . . on grounds of a few tenants who apparently cannot be accommodated." Aside from the fact that the "few tenants" actually constitute the majority of people (namely all women plus some men from particular racial-ethnic groups), imagine the reverse situation: a general theory of social ascription that regrettably does not apply to men. I doubt that many social scientists would hesitate to remove it as a cornerstone of theory even though its nonapplicability to "a few" male tenants was its only drawback. We cannot point to an example of this reverse case because a general theory that did not apply to men would never gain the status of a general theory; hence there is no need to dislodge it.

A less obvious form of using a male frame of reference occurs when events are evaluated by their effects on males only. For instance, the Rennaissance is commonly regarded as a progressive

era in Western civilization. It was, however, a time during which
women lost many of the privileges they had enjoyed during the
period of chivalry.[4] This era appears "progressive" only when one
considers its effects on men but not on women.

2.2.2 *Construction of the Actor as Male*

This aspect of androcentricity constructs the actor as male only.
When females are considered at all in such a context, they appear
as objects, as acted upon, rather than as coactors.

Looking at a recent article on sociobiology in the *Canadian Review
of Sociology and Anthropology*, we find the following statement:

> Do ritualized aggression and lethal conflict serve similar functions
> among humans? Alcock ... concludes that most threatening or
> violent disputes are employed to resolve contested ownership over
> scarce or potentially limiting resources. ... Sociologist Van den
> Berghe ... interprets intergroup warfare as a rational means of
> gaining livestock, women and slaves, gaining or keeping territory, or
> gaining, controlling and exploiting new territory.[5]

In this statement, "intergroup warfare" is defined as warfare among
males of different groups, while women are among the resources to
be gained or controlled (after livestock and before slaves). In other
words, women are not conceptualized as group members; if they
were, their presumed nonparticipation in warfare would need
some comment and consideration. If, upon investigation, it turned
out that women did not in fact actively participate in "intergroup
warfare," then clearly the term is a misnomer. A more appropriate
label might be "warfare among males of different groups" or simply
"male intergroup warfare," which would at least make clear the fact
that only one sex is engaging in this practice. Such identification
also raises the question of what the relationships among the
women of different groups might have been like – and if, why, and
how they were different from those of males. Presumably, at this
point, a scholar would then propose a *general* theory, as opposed to
a sex-specific theory, of "intergroup warfare."

Such an analysis of the meaning of concepts is not mere

quibbling over words, as becomes obvious when one pursues this issue further. Sticking for the moment with the same topic and author, we find in a different article in the same journal issue statements about the "proximate causes and seeds of warfare."[6] In trying to explain warfare, the author examines group cohesiveness and argues:

> In our work, the axiom of inclusive fitness provides a raison d'etre for group membership since individuals have a genetic interest in kin fitness. Groups serve as organizational vehicles in which individuals can monitor, and if necessary protect, the fitness of related members, having subsequent bearing on their own inclusive fitness. The more cohesive the group, the more members can effectively assess their inclusive fitness. In this respect, inclusive fitness would predispose genetically related individuals to band together beyond, say, the extended family.[7]

In addition to a genetic interest, the author also hypothesizes that environmental factors are important. His speculation runs as follows:

> In early hominid evolution, membership in an expanded group would likely have increased each individual's access to scarce resources and ability to manage others. Hunting in numbers, for example, would have enabled primitive man to overcome large game. Numbers would also have reduced susceptibility of individuals to attack by predators. To facilitate hunting and prevent attack, groups would almost certainly have served as information centres for defining and locating resources and predators. The more these features of group membership enhanced inclusive fitness (the rate of reproduction, quality of offspring, survival), the more group members would have been deterred from splintering off. In short, the social behavior of early humans probably was structured largely by both defense against large predators and competition with them.....[8]

At first glance, these two passages, seem perfectly nonsexist, except for one lapse in language, the reference to "primitive man." If the passage were meant to apply to both sexes, the term would be overspecific. As it turns out, however, the term is quite literally correct, because the passages talk only about primitive man and not primitive woman.

On a previous page of the article, the existence of an incest taboo was implicitly accepted.[9] Presumably this means that women, who, after all, are needed to improve the inclusive fitness of a group, typically are not from the same group as the males with whom they mate. In other words, the various groups presumably practiced some form of exogamy. In the first cited article, we found that women might be obtained through intergroup warfare of males.

This means that the concept of "group cohesion" applies only to males and not to females, since typically the females would join, for mating purposes, a group other than the one into which they were born. In such a case, approximately half of the group members were not banding together beyond the extended family in order to increase their inclusive fitness. Where does this leave the entire theory?

Turning to the second paragraph quoted, the prevailing assumption is that large game hunting was an exclusively male activity. Therefore, the statement that "groups served as information centres" about predators is obviously again about male groups and not mixed-sex groups. At best, then, the statements can be half true – applicable to one half of the population only. In that case, it is surely inappropriate to make the statements in as general and imperative a form as the one in which they presently appear.

Other concepts in general use in anthropology are also sometimes constructed with ego defined as male. To provide one more example from this same article, the author suggests that early human history can be divided into three periods of sociality, all of which involve (variously small or large) "polygynous, probably multi-male bands."[10] Polygyny (having many wives) is a concept in which ego is constructed as male. A female version would be "husband sharing," "joint husbands," or the like. However, it is the combination of the term "polygynous" with "multi-male" that establishes the male reference in a particularly clear manner, and which relegates women to the status of nonactors. If the males are polygynous, the groups are not only multi-male, but also multi-female. However, by having defined women only as wives, and not as actors or group members in their own right, they become completely invisible, as is evidenced in the following passage:

one of the first evolutionary steps taken as weapons developed was to severely restrict individuals from changing groups. From the resident's point of view, the admission of an extragroup conspecific would lead to now dangerous rank-order confrontations. The closing of hominid groups would have resulted in two beneficial effects from the standpoint of inclusive fitness. First, because males increasingly tended to remain in their natal group the genetic interrelatedness among the adult males, and in the group as a whole, would increase. This would have increased solidarity among group members and thus cohesion of the group per se.[11]

Once more, it is obvious that the group is conceptualized as consisting of males who have assorted wives who have no effect whatsoever on group cohesion and solidarity. The "individual" and the "resident" are *male* individuals and residents, not females, since women *did* change groups. The possibility of rank-order confrontations among women, and their possible consequences, is not even considered relevant, since in effect women have been defined as unimportant in the context of the group.

So far, our examples of androcentricity have been taken from one author and from one particular approach to the social sciences. As with all other types of sexism, constructing the actor as male is a practice that is found in a wide variety of approaches, authors, and disciplines. For example, to stay for a moment with the concept of polygyny, we find a definition of it, in quite a different context, as a description of concubinage in Anglo-Saxon England:

A man might have a plurality of sexual partners, specifically where one of these is a legal spouse and the other a concubine with customary privileges but without legal recognition. Alternatively, we are concerned with cases in which a man has no legal sexual partner but a publicly recognized consort. These circumstances are more accurately defined by the term concubinage than polygyny, which actually refers to a situation in which a man is permitted to have more than one wife at a time on a fully legal basis, though it is rare for the several wives to share equal social status.[12]

This definition is not wrong, but it is clearly one-sided and created from the perspective of one sex despite the fact that polygyny concerns both sexes equally. What would the definition look like from the perspective of women? Clearly, it would read quite differently: it would also be more complicated, because we would need to distinguish between the wives and the concubines as well as take into consideration wives with monogamous husbands (those who do not avail themselves of the opportunity of having multiple sexual partners even though this would be socially acceptable).

It is often the entire concept of society that is conceptualized in androcentric terms. One such instance of an androcentric vision appears again in the stratification literature. In discussing function-alist approaches to stratification, this author asks rhetorically:

> Is stratification, then, necessary for placement and motivation? It is not logically necessary, of course, or this aspect of the theory would be true by definition, rather than empirically testable and potentially falsifiable. It is possible that people of talent might undertake the training required for functionally important positions and fulfill their duties without differentials in extrinsic rewards, perhaps moved to do so by "alternative motivational schemes." ... Individuals could be socialized to think of it as their self-rewarding duty, for example, to take on important tasks and to do them well, as in the notion of noblesse oblige. ... Unfortunately, however, we seem to lack convincing contemporary or historical examples of societies with such alternative motivational schemes.[13]

The statement that we lack examples of such "alternative motivational schemes" ignores one of the most important functional tasks of all times, peoples, and strata: care of the young. For centuries women have fulfilled this vital task (and how many other tasks can truly be called vital?) due not to extrinsic rewards but to an "alternative motivational scheme." Ignoring what women have done thus leads to a misinterpretation on a grand scale.

To give one final example, the concept of the suburb as a "bedroom community" conceptualizes the entire population of the suburbs in terms of those people who leave in the morning to go to their paid work. At the time at which this concept emerged, it meant primarily employed males. Most women, practically all children, and some men would remain in the suburbs. For them, therefore, the suburbs did not serve as a bedroom community.[14]

In the above examples we can see that constructing ego as male not only leads easily to the portrayal of women as passive, as those acted upon, but it also sometimes results in their complete invisibility. On the other hand, it is important not to commit the error of assuming agency or activity on the part of women in cases in which it is inappropriate. This problem is discussed in sections 2.2.5 and 2.2.6.

2.2.3 *Gynopia or Female Invisibility*

To illustrate gynopia, or female invisibility, we move to economics, to an article on "The Demand for Unobservable and Other Nonpositional Goods."[15] The author defines positional goods as

> those things whose value depends relatively strongly on how they compare with things owned by others. Goods that depend relatively less strongly on such comparisons will be called nonpositional goods. As noted, the nonpositional category includes, but is not limited to, goods that are not readily observed by outsiders.[16]

This article rests on the premise that useful insights into people's economic behavior can be gained by the view that the utility function (or what psychologists would call the structure of motivation) is shaped by the forces of natural selection. In order to clarify his point, the author presents an example of an individual, A, who is concerned about his children. He discusses his choice of work environment, his feelings, his ranking in the income hierarchy, his level of ability, his work for his true marginal product, his ability to devote more of his resources to the purchase of "x," and so on. The following quotation gives a taste of the completely male connotations:

> If people are certain of their rank in the positional goods hierarchy, the model as it is expressed above does not produce a stable outcome. The lowest-ranking member of the hierarchy could initially move past the second-lowest ranking member by increasing his consumption of positional goods; and the second lowest-ranking member could then restore the original ordering by carrying out a similar shift of his own. But then the lowest-ranking member could

reduce his consumption of positional goods without adversely affecting his ranking, which would already be as low as it could get. In turn, the second lowest-ranking member could then reduce *his* consumption of nonpositional goods without penalty, and in like fashion the high-ranking members would one-by-one have an incentive to follow suit.[17]

There are two ways in which this passage can be interpreted. One could assume that it simply employs sexist language by using the male term as a generic term, in which case we are dealing with an instance of overgeneralization at the level of language. Alternatively, the reference is truly exclusively male and is not meant to be applicable to women. In the example given above, we seem to be dealing with the latter case, as is evidenced by the author's statement that "the average length of job tenure is much higher for union than for nonunion members"[18] and his supporting footnote:

> Jacob Mincer . . . finds, for example, that quit rates in the union sector are about one-half as large as in the nonunion sector for young men and about one-third as large for men over 30.[19]

Similarly, he backs up his statement that "we also know that union members earn significantly higher wages than do nonunion workers with comparable job skills"[20] with the footnote:

> Mincer . . . for example, finds ability-adjusted union wage premiums of 6–14 percent for men under 30, and 4–12 percent for older men.[21]

The fact that the author's evidence is strictly applicable to males does not lead him to reflect on whether his generalizations are equally applicable to women, nor does it lead him to indicate in the title of his article that he is really only discussing the demand for unobservable and nonpositional goods for males.

Similar criticisms have been made of the discipline of history and the work of specific historians. For example, as Ruth Pierson and Alison Prentice point out:

The eminent socialist historian Eric Hobsbawm failed to include women in his 1971 theoretical plea for a social history so all-encompassing that it would become a history of all society.[22] In 1978, he admitted the justness of the criticism "that male historians in the past, including marxists, have grossly neglected the female half of the human race," and included himself among the culprits. . . . Another example of bias is Philippe Aries' path-breaking study of the history of childhood, which deals almost exclusively with male children.[23]

2.2.4 *The Maintenance of Male over Female Interests*

Maintaining male over female interests may take various forms. One of them is a trivializing of problems experienced by women at the hands of men. An example of this can be found in a recent publication of Statistics Canada, *Divorce: Law and the Family in Canada.*[24] For instance, when discussing grounds for divorce, the authors start out by noting that

> it would appear that the bases of divorce vary with the sex of the players. In Table 6 it is apparent that women petitioners select grounds different from those habitually chosen by men.[25]

Just considering, for a moment, the grammar of this sentence, it would seem reasonable to assume that men petition for divorce more often than women, or at least that men and women petition for divorce with approximately the same frequency, since women are compared with men rather than the other way around. However, looking at the table this sentence refers to, we find that the authors are discussing 330,740 wives who have petitioned for divorce as opposed to only 173,890 husbands who petitioned for divorce.

The paragraph cited above then continues:

> The principal category for both sexes is noncohabitation. However, it is more popular with men since they rely on it half the time while women petitioners rely on it just over a third (37%) of the time. Men also use adultery considerably more often than women: 36.6% as compared to 27.5%. However, in both cases, adultery is the second most often pleaded ground.

As we have already noted, men rarely (5.4%) plead grounds of mental and/or physical cruelty. Rather mental and/or physical cruelty are "female" grounds invoked by women petitioners far more frequently (19.0%) than men. . . .

Generally, men use adultery or noncohabitation (85.5%) and although women use these grounds as well, they make much more use of the remaining possibilities. These differences may be due to fundamental differences between men and women or they may simply reflect that more grounds are easily used by women than men. We have already discussed this likelihood with reference to mental and physical cruelty. It also seems plausible that such grounds as imprisonment, rape, and alcohol or narcotics addiction are much more easily used by women even though in general, these grounds are not heavily relied on. Essentially adultery and noncohabitation seem the only two particularly effective choices available to men. In addition, these two grounds are the easiest to prove.[26]

Contrast this discussion with the fact that 66 percent of all divorce petitions are made by women, not men, as the table that is being discussed shows. It seems that the only important grounds for divorce are those cited by men, and that women "choose" other grounds because they "use them more easily" than men. There is no recognition that perhaps the differential grounds for divorce may reflect differential behavior of women and men during marriage. Such reflection would, of course, be less than flattering to men, since it suggests that men are much more likely to abuse their wives mentally or physically – as indeed other studies confirm[27] – than women are to abuse their husbands.

Nor is the incidence of cruelty so low. When we combine the cases in which wives petition for divorce in which cruelty is cited as either the sole reason or as one factor among others, we find that 29.9 percent of all female petitions, or 98,892 cases, in the years under consideration cited cruelty as a ground for divorce, compared to 173,890 men who petitioned for divorce for *any* reason whatsoever. It is hardly adequate, under these circumstances, to conclude:

Although there are 15 individual grounds for divorce, most divorcing Canadians rely on only three: cruelty, adultery or separation for not less than three years. . . . The first two are fault-oriented and together account for 44.9% of all cases, while the latter (noncohabitation) places an emphasis on marriage failure, accounting for 41.0% of all cases.

These grounds are differentially invoked by men and women – men rely on noncohabitation and tend to ignore cruelty, while women use cruelty more often although their most often chosen category of grounds is also noncohabitation (separation).[28]

"Men tend to ignore cruelty" while "women use cruelty more often" is comparable to arguing that some crime victims choose to press charges for stealing, while others prefer to press charges for assault. Descriptions of this type trivialize a very substantial problem that women experience at the hands of men. They thus constitute euphemistic descriptions of male behavior. By failing to identify a social problem as such, they implicitly serve male over female interests.

Another example of the same type of problem can be found in an anthropological study of *Yanomamo: The Fierce People*.[29] The author, Napoleon Chagnon, provides innumerable examples of male violence among the Yanomamo. Wife abuse predominates in their everyday existence. Warfare is often conducted as a means of abducting women in order for the men of a particular clan to acquire more wives. Rape is part of this abduction, and men are considered to be perfectly within their rights to beat their wives for the slightest provocation, such as when the wife is slow in preparing a meal. Chagnon discusses and illustrates wife abuse throughout his text, yet there is only one paragraph describing how the women perceive this abuse, and this is based on an overheard conversation.

Women expect this kind of treatment and many of them measure their husband's concern in terms of the frequency of the minor beatings they sustain. I overheard two young women discussing their scalp scars. One of them commented that the other's husband must really care for her since he had beaten her on the head so frequently.[30]

Chagnon bases his interpretation of the women's general attitude on only one overheard conversation. He never directly asks any of the women how they felt. Furthermore, by inserting the term "minor beatings" into his analysis, he makes a judgment that may be quite inappropriate, given that the woman received scalp scars as a result. There are many other examples of sexism in this book, but trivializing male abuse of females is one clear instance of placing male interests above female interests.

Another form of maintaining male over female interests can be found in a recent report of the Economic Council of Canada.[31] In this annual review, the Council included, for the first time ever, a special chapter on Women and Work. It therefore warrants some attention.

The Council documents, in two separate tables, the rather gross earnings differentials between women and men in the twenty highest and twenty lowest paid occupations for 1970 and 1981. The Council then comments on these tables as follows:

> Within both the highest- and the lowest-paid activities there has been some progress in narrowing the female/male earnings gap. When adjusted for hours worked per year, the gaps narrow; and it seems likely that they would narrow still further if they were adjusted for education and experience. Nevertheless, the gaps remain very wide. This suggests that the principle of equal pay for equal or equivalent work must continue to be enforced vigorously. Yet, if there is to be further substantial improvement in the relative earnings of women, the issue goes beyond that to more basic questions of training related to market needs, the balancing of family and career aspirations, and greater occupational diversification. Progress is being made, but slowly, and mostly by the young. Among older women who lack the specialized training needed for many of today's better-paid jobs, the route has been more difficult.[32]

These comments are truly ironic, for two reasons. The report identifies the following as the "more basic questions": training related to market needs, the balancing of family and career aspirations, and greater occupational diversification. But the comparisons made are *within* occupations, where appropriate training presumably exists; this sample thus represents women who *have* contributed to female diversification (since they *are* in the highest-paid jobs); and the report fails to mention that the wage differentials are significantly higher (both in an absolute as well as in a relative sense) in the highest- not the lowest-paid occupations.

The summary further neglects to alert us to the fact that in some of these jobs women actually lost ground in a relative sense vis-á-vis men: for 16 percent of the women in the highest-paid occupations (namely for directors general, optometrists, veterinarians, university teachers, members of legislative bodies, administrators – teaching, and air transport foremen), the wage differential *increased* between 1970 and 1980. For women in the lowest-paid occupations, the gap increased by 11 percent: Women working as babysitters; workers on farms; in horticulture and animal husbandry; in occupations in fishing, hunting, and trapping; and as barbers and hairdressers lost ground to men. Taking all occupations considered into account, it remains true that for the majority of women in both the highest- and lowest-paid occupations, the wage gap decreased somewhat.

However, another table informs us that if we control hourly earnings by education level, men with less education consistently make more than do women with more education.[33] Thus a man with secondary schooling or less makes more than a woman with a nonuniversity diploma or certificate or some university training, while a man with similar educational qualifications makes more than does a woman with a bachelor's degree or certificate; in turn, a man with a bachelor's degree makes more than does a woman with a postgraduate degree. These figures suggest forcefully that the problem is *not* primarily one of training, for with the same amount of training, women make substantially lower hourly wages. (This means that the overall wage difference cannot be explained by the fact that women may potentially work fewer hours than men because the comparison is based on *hourly*, not weekly or monthly, earnings).

In its conclusions, the report recommends adequacy in terms of alternative forms of child care, pension rights for women, and encouragement for women and girls, "along with young men, to acquire nontraditional skills that will facilitate wider occupational choice in subsequent years" (p. 107). While there is nothing wrong with these recommendations and the previously cited recommendations, they nevertheless do not address the fact that women and men *within the same occupations* experience wide income gaps. What is conspicuous by its absence is a recommendation to pursue vigorously a program of equal pay for work of equal value, which is referred to in the text passage cited above as a principle that "must continue to be enforced vigorously."

All else remaining equal, given that women with the same educational level have significantly lower hourly earnings than men, educational programs alone will *not* eliminate the wage gap, although they may have other beneficial effects. By focusing on educational achievements rather than on systemic wage differentials, however, this analysis diverts attention from a significant structural problem. Instead, it assesses the chief difficulty as an individual problem: get a better education and reconsider your family commitments, if you are a woman (apparently this is not necessary if you are a man), and your problems will disappear. The only drawback to this advice is that, as the report documents, heeding it will not make the problems disappear.

2.2.5 Misogyny and Blaming Women

Maintaining male over female interests may take the extreme form of outright misogyny (that is, hatred of women) and blaming women. These two phenomena are so closely related that they can be treated as one and the same, since very often blaming women takes the form of blaming them for the fact that they (or their children) are victimized. This is especially true when the discussion concerns sexual violence: from a misogynistic perspective, sexual violence against women (and children) is implicitly justified (that is, the victims deserve to be victimized); thus the woman is "blamed" for her victimization and becomes not the victim but the accused. Such bias may be blatant (as in the above example) or subtle, but in any case, it constitutes the adoption of a male perspective and thus is an instance of androcentricity.

Our first example comes from the journal *Child Development*.[34] The article deals with "seductive mother-toddler relationships." One must first of all ask oneself to whom the described behaviors are seductive? To the infant? To the mother? Or to the adult (male or female) observer who applies the standards of an adult male?

Seductive behavior is described as follows:

At times this took the form of certain kinds of physical contact (squeezing the buttocks, stroking the stomach, and even grabbing the genital area). At other times it involved sensual teasing, a plaintive voice, or promises of affection if the child would comply. In all cases these behaviours were viewed as seductive, not because they were intended to lead to frank sexual contact, but because "in addition to being insensitive and unresponsive to the needs of the child, they [drew] the child into patterns of interaction that are overly stimulating and role inappropriate." ... The behaviour involved either physical contact motivated by the mother's needs, rather than by the child's, or manipulating the child using sensuality. In no case was it responsive to bids by the toddler.[35]

It is important to note that in *no* case were the behaviors intended to lead to frank sexual contact. Their classification as "seductive" therefore does *not* derive from the actual context but from extrapolation of what these behaviors would mean were they addressed to an adult male. A better term might be "manipulative sensuality" or simply "excessive control and manipulation."

The language in this study vacillates between being specific and being overgeneral. A good example is provided in the following section, where we find that "parent-child relationships" in fact refer to mother-child relationships, and even more specifically, often (but not always) to mother-son relationships:

We are interested in understanding parent-child relationship systems, including the relation between one parent-child relationship and the relationship between that parent and another child. If particular qualities of parent-child relationships can be defined, we may explore whether distinct but predictable qualities likely characterize the relationships of that parent with other children in the family. Where the mother is seductive with her son, what is the nature of her relationship with her daughter? Were one not investigating a sample of largely single mothers, such as ours, spouse and father-child relations also could be included.[36]

It is in the context of this "sample of largely single mothers" that the inappropriateness of the term "seductive maternal behavior" becomes particularly clear. In view of the mounting evidence that many males do indeed engage in "frank sexual contact" with their children, it seems highly ironic to identify behavior that does *not* lead to such contact with a term that indicates that it does.

This lopsidedness becomes upsettingly clear when one reads through the entire article. The authors state that

> we believe that seductive behaviour towards a child, and dissolution of generational boundaries more generally, is a reflection of the parent's relationship history and ongoing needs. A parent behaves seductively toward a child because their own needs for nurturance have been unmet and because they learned in childhood that parents may attempt to meet their own emotional needs through their children.[37]

Presumably, all the parents that are being discussed here are in fact mothers. Talking about parents rather than mothers in this context is singularly inappropriate (underspecific) when sex is such a crucial variable. We learn later, quite a bit later than the passage just cited, that

> interview data concerning incest history were compared for 19 mothers having "high generational boundary" dissolution scores ... with the other 170 mothers in the sample. While only 8% of the larger sample reported a history of being sexually abused in the family, 42% of the target mothers reported such experiences.[38]

Forty-two percent of the "target mothers" suffered from incest, but they do *not* themselves engage in incest. Instead, the "seductive" behavior, inappropriate though it may be, seems relatively harmless when compared with incest.

The scale for measuring the dissolution of generational boundaries in this study

> was designed to capture an age-related transformation of the seductive patterns that was more far-reaching [than nonresponsive intimacy]. The broader issue of generational boundary dissolution may be manifest other than in strictly physical terms. Mother and child may behave as peers, mother may defer to the child for

direction (role reversal), or mother may be charmed and amused by the child at the expense of providing the direction he needs. For example, the child deliberately misplaces a shape. Mother clucks her tongue and laughingly says, "What are you doing now, you devil, you?" Then they both put their head on the table and giggle.[39]

It is this type of "dissolution of generational boundaries" that constitutes a "more far-reaching" transformation of the seductive pattern, but both this and incest (of the adult male with the female child) are termed "boundary dissolution." Clearly the term trivializes the male assault and problematizes comparatively harmless female behavior.

The general androcentric bias of this study is blatantly obvious in other concepts employed. For instance, the authors state:

> One might predict that mothers would be concordant for seductive behaviour with male siblings (a style of relating to boys) but not opposite-sex siblings, where there would be no relation.[40]

Here we encounter the curious constructions of "male siblings" and "opposite-sex siblings." Siblings to whom? Clearly to the male child. Everybody else is – most of the time but not always – described in relation to this male child, rather than in terms reciprocal to one another. Moreover, "target dyads" are described as "mother-sister dyads,"[41] as compared to "target other-male dyads" and "target mother-sister dyads."[42] Who is the implied referent in this set of concepts? Not the mother, because if so, the dyads would have been identified as mother-son and mother-daughter dyads (mother-son is, in fact, sometimes used).

The authors note toward the end of their article that

> the results distinguish the construct we are defining from a generalized seductiveness concept. There was not concordance in seductive behavior across siblings. While it certainly may be the case that some mothers are seductive with more than one son, not one such case emerged in our data, and the other findings of this study suggest that mothers are unlikely to be seductive with sons and daughters alike.[43]

Note the continuing androcentricity: Whose siblings? One might suspect that siblings are seductive among themselves if it were not for the overall context of the article. In addition the substantive statement contained in this passage underlines the inappropriateness of the term "seductive behavior," which in effect equates incest with a wide range of possibly inappropriate but less serious behaviors. In no case did a mother engage in truly sexual behavior, and in no case was more than one child involved, while men often *do* sexually abuse their children and grandchildren and often abuse more than one child.

The entire area of sexual abuse is one in which sexist theories predominate. Judith Herman, in an overview of various theories on sexual abuse of children, has noted that

> the doctor, the man of letters, and the pornographer, each in his accustomed language, render similar judgements of the incestuous father's mate. By and large, they suggest, she drove him to it. The indictment of the mother includes three counts: first, she failed to perform her marital duties; second, she, not the father, forced the daughter to take her rightful place; and third, she knew about, tolerated, or in some cases actively enjoyed the incest.[44]

Diana E. H. Russell comments on this passage:

> It has been easier to blame mothers than to face the fact that daughters are vulnerable to sexual abuse when they do not have strong mothers to protect them from their own fathers and other male relatives. But mothers should not have to protect their children from their children's fathers! And a mother's "failure" to protect her child should not be seen as a causative factor in child sexual abuse.[45]

What we see, then, is the tendency to accuse women of inappropriate or negligent – sometimes even criminal – sexual behavior with their children, when it is men who, statistically, are the real abusers. Women suddenly emerge as active rather than passive, just at the moment when blame is being assigned for the sexual mistreatment of children.

2.2.6 Defending Female Subjugation or
Male Dominance

Mary Daly, in her book *Gyn/Ecology*,[46] provides a detailed analysis of
several forms of female subjugation, mutilation, and degradation in
different cultures and at different times, including the Indian rite of
suttee (widow-burning), the Chinese custom of footbinding, and
African customs of genital mutilation. She also shows clearly that
many scholars implicitly or explicitly have defended such rites,
which result in horrible suffering or death for women. There is no
need to repeat this analysis here, but let us consider one example
from Daly's work:

> If the general situation of widowhood in India was not a sufficient
> inducement for the woman of higher caste to throw herself gratefully
> and ceremoniously into the fire, she was often pushed and poked in
> with long stakes after having been bathed, ritually attired, and
> drugged out of her mind. In case these facts should interfere with our
> clear misunderstanding of the situation, Webster's invites us to re-
> *cover* women's history with the following definition of *suttee*: "the act
> or custom of a Hindu woman *willingly* cremating herself or being
> cremated on the funeral pyre of her husband as an indication of her
> *devotion* to him [emphases by Daly]." It is thought-provoking to
> consider the reality behind the term *devotion*, for indeed a wife must
> have shown signs of extraordinarily slavish devotion during her
> husband's lifetime, since her very life depended upon her husband's
> state of health.[47]

My later edition of Webster's[48] defines suttee as "a Hindu widow
who immolates herself on the funeral pile of her husband; the
voluntary self-immolation by fire of a Hindu widow."

2.3 Manifestations of Androcentricity in the Research Process

2.3.1 Androcentricity in Language

Most forms of sexism in language fall under the general rubric of overgeneralization/overspecificity and are therefore considered in the following chapter. However, one aspect of this problem is properly identified as falling into the area of androcentricity: the sequencing of the sexes. It is impossible to avoid mentioning one sex first when both are considered; this is not an issue at all if there is some reasonable alternation as to which sex gets mentioned first. However, if one sex is consistently mentioned first (for example, by combinations of "men and women" or "he and she" or "Mr. and Mrs. Smith"), and such combinations are elevated to the level of grammatical rules, a mild form of androcentricity results. Conversely, if the mention of females consistently precedes that of males, a mild form of gynocentricity results. (I did not encounter any examples of the latter form of bias, and therefore the problem is identified solely as one of androcentricity).

2.3.2 Androcentric (and Gynocentric) Concepts

One important way in which concepts can be sexist occurs when the concept includes a hidden one-sex referent. For example, the concept of the suburb as a "bedroom community" has as a referent the working adult male who leaves the suburb in the morning to return in the evening. For women who are housewives or who work in the neighborhood as waitresses, in beauty salons, as bank tellers, or as teachers (and for children who attend a neighborhood school, go to a day care center, or stay at home), the suburb is definitely *not* a bedroom community.

Two other examples of androcentric concepts are those of "group cohesion," which, as defined in sociobiology, focuses exclusively on the males within a group; and "intergroup warfare," which in fact refers to males of different groups who battle against each other.

Likewise, the concept of polygyny (many wives) refers to the male who has multiple wives, rather than to the female who shares her husband. An equivalent female term might be "husband sharing." An anthropological study about "husband sharing" would certainly be organized quite differently than one about "polygyny." Of course, the concept of polyandry (many husbands) has a female referent; here the corresponding male term might be "wife sharing."

Another way in which androcentricity appears in concepts is the inclusion of a demeaning attribute with a sex indicator, as in the concept of the "masochistic woman." Paula Caplan offers this analysis:

> What . . . is the behavior that in women has led to their being called masochistic? Much of it is in fact *learned* behavior, the very essence of femininity in Western culture. Girls and women are supposed to be nurturant, selfless (even self-denying), and endlessly patient. What often goes hand in hand with these traits is low self-esteem. Since no one with decent self-respect would be endlessly nurturant and consider it unnatural to want something for herself, society must train women to believe that without their nurturant behavior, without what they can give to another person, they are nothing. . . .
>
> Once females have been trained in this way, and act nurturant, charitable, and compassionate, this behavior is then labeled masochistic.[49]

The reverse form of this bias would be the use of misandrist concepts (that is, terms that include a demeaning attribute with a male sex indicator). I did not find any examples of this within the literature that I examined, nor could I or friends and colleagues whom I asked recall any. This fact in and of itself says something about the state of the literature. Nevertheless, it does not rule out the possibility that misandrist concepts may exist.

2.3.3 Androcentricity in the Research Design

A very pervasive way in which research can be androcentric is through an androcentric perspective that shapes an entire study. The previously discussed example from sociobiology concerning warfare in "primitive man" provides one such example. The problems are defined from a male perspective, and the variables examined are those that affect men, while those affecting women are ignored. There is no discussion, for example, of whether group cohesion was generated in women through joint nursing of children. In this specific case, both the overall research question and specific questions addressed to the data are so intertwined that they cannot be meaningfully separated from each other. In other instances, only specific questions addressed to respondents can be identified as androcentric.

A broader issue emerges when we consider the cumulative effect of androcentricity in many studies within an area (as opposed to the androcentric bias of one particular study). Scholarly research is supposed to be embedded within its appropriate literature. If an entire area has been shaped by androcentric research (as is likely to often be the case), it is necessary to consider the area carefully as a whole and ask oneself whether, for instance, the variables considered important include those that are particularly important for women. Many feminist critiques of traditional ways of "doing history" center on this issue.

The reverse problem occurs when researchers identify as female an activity in which both women and men participate. One noted family researcher found it necessary to emphasize that "clearly, the terms *family* and *mother-child interaction* are not the same."[50] He continues, "Gradually, in studies of family behavior, fathers are being admitted as participants, but most investigators have not begun to treat families as empirical entities."[51]

An androcentric focus may also be a problem even when a researcher plans to include both males and females in a study. If the area of research is one from which women traditionally have been excluded from consideration,[52] it may be necessary to plan an exploratory pilot study (prior to the main study) to assess the adequacy of the variables normally used in this type of research.

2.3.4 Validation of Research Instrument

If a research instrument is developed and validated for one sex only and is then used for the other sex, it cannot be considered validated. For example, if a research instrument is developed and validated on males but used on both sexes, it introduces an androcentric bias. Such was the case with Kohlberg's famous model of the development of moral judgment, which he derived from an empirical study of eighty-four boys whose development he followed for a period of over twenty years.[53] Another well-known example of this source of bias is the widely used distinction between "instrumental" and "expressive" leaders, which was developed by observing the behavior of male undergraduate students,[54] and was subsequently used to describe the proper roles for husbands (instrumental leaders) and wives (expressive leaders).[55] Similarly, if an instrument were developed and validated using females only and were then applied to both females and males, it would introduce a gynocentric bias.

2.3.5 *Formulation of Questions and Questionnaires*

We have already noted that research questions may be biased in a number of ways. Here we are concerned with the actual questions posed to respondents, such as in survey research, qualitative interviews, or opinion polls, where a single question may be posed to respondents. An androcentric bias may appear in the manner in which questions are formulated.

For instance, where the intent of a question is to compare attitudes about males and females with respect to some capacity, questions are sometimes formulated so that one sex or the other serves as the norm against which the other is measured (thus eliminating the possibility for surpassing the normative sex). Take, for example, the following statements (respondents were asked to agree or disagree with them):

- It is generally better to have a man at the head of a department composed of both men and women employees.
- It is acceptable for women to hold important political offices in state and national government.[56]

In these cases female heads of departments or female incumbents of important political offices are measured against the norm established by male incumbents. The wording of the statements makes it impossible for the respondent to indicate that he or she might see female department heads or office holders as *preferable*. Thus only half of the possible spectrum of responses is allowed for.

The items could, of course, be rephrased to allow for the full range of possible responses:

- What do you think is generally better: To have a woman or a man at the head of a department that is composed of both men and women employees?

- . . . to have women or men hold important elected political offices in state and national government?

Permissible responses to such items could then be:

- It is much better to have a man.
- It is somewhat better to have a man.
- It makes no difference.
- It is somewhat better to have a woman.
- It is much better to have a woman.

2.4 Conclusion

Androcentricity takes many forms, including a male viewpoint or frame of reference, the construction of an actor as male, female invisibility, misogyny and blaming women, and the defense of cultural practices that directly subjugate or harm women. These various manifestations are, of course, not independent of one another. We can think of them as different facets of the same phenomenon.

Androcentricity may manifest itself in all components of the research process, but the two most important manifestations are in concepts and in the overall research design. It is thus not easy to eliminate. We need to step out of the accepted mode of thinking to ask ourselves: Does this concept or research design address the concerns and viewpoints of women and men equally? If not, a new approach is called for.

Such a new approach can be called a "dual perspective," as opposed to a single (male) perspective. In the absence of a female perspective that is developed as well as a male perspective, applying a dual perspective necessarily involves reinvestigating issues about which we thought we already knew enough.

We need to create baseline data sets that are comparable for women and men. This will mean, for quite a while, putting special emphasis on studying women rather than men, in order to start redressing the current imbalance. It also implies looking at both men and women from a female rather than a male perspective. Both sexes must be understood as gendered people. In the process, we will learn new things not only about women, but about men as well.

Notes

1 Simone de Beauvoir, *The Second Sex* (New York: Bantam, 1972). See also Jean Bethke Elshtain, "Women as mirror and other: Toward a theory of women, war, and feminism," *Humanities in Society* 5, 1/2 (1982): 29–44.

2 Shulamit Reinharz, "Feminist distrust: Problems of context and content in sociological work," in David N. Berg and Kenwyn K. Smith (eds.), *Exploring Clinical Methods for Social Research* (Beverly Hills, CA: Sage, 1985): 153–172, quote on p. 170.

3 Alfred A. Hunter, *Class Tells: On Social Inequality in Canada*, 2nd ed. (Toronto: Butterworths, 1986): 185. It should be noted that in spite of the formulation of this paragraph, this author is one of the sharpest critics of the human capital approach, precisely because of its sexism; see Margaret A. Denton and Alfred A. Hunter, *Equality in the Workplace: Economic Sectors and Gender Discrimination in Canada: A Critique and Test of Block and Walker . . . and Some New Evidence.* Women's Bureau, Ser. A, No. 6 (Ottawa:Labour Canada, 1984).

4 Edward B. Fiske, "Scholars face a challenge by feminists," *New York Times* (Nov. 23, 1981): 1.

5 R. Paul Shaw, "Humanity's propensity for warfare: A sociobiological perspective," *Canadian Review of Sociology and Anthropology* 22, 2 (1985): 158–183, quote on p. 166.

6 R. Paul Shaw, "Merging ultimate and proximate causes in sociobiology and studies of warfare," *Canadian Review of Sociology and Anthropology* 22, 2 (1985): 192–201.

7 Ibid., p. 196.

8 Ibid.
9 Ibid., p. 195.
10 Ibid., p. 197.
11 Ibid., pp. 197–198.
12 Margaret Clunies Ross, "Concubinage in Anglo-Saxon England," *Past and Present* 108 (1985): 3–34, quote on p. 6.
13 Hunter, *Class Tells*, p. 33.
14 Lyn H. Lofland, "The 'thereness' of women": A selective review of urban sociology," in Marcia Millman and Rosabeth Moss Kanter (eds.), *Another Voice* (Garden City, NY: Anchor, 1975): 144–170.
15 Robert H. Frank, "The demand for unobservable and other nonpositional goods," *American Economic Review* 75, 1 (1985): 101–116.
16 Ibid., p. 101.
17 Ibid., p. 106.
18 Ibid., p. 111.
19 Ibid., p. 111, fn. 15.
20 Ibid., p. 111.
21 Ibid., p. 111, fn. 18.
22 E. J. Hobsbawm, "From social history to the history of society," in Felix Gilbert and Stephen R. Graubard (eds.), *Historical Studies Today* (New York: Norton, 1971): 1–26.
23 Ruth Pierson and Alison Prentice, "Feminism and the writing and teaching of history," in Angela Miles and Geraldine Finn (eds.), *Feminism in Canada: From Pressure to Politics* (Montreal: Black Rose, 1982): 103–118, quote on p. 109.
24 D. C. McKie, B. Prentice, and P. Reed. *Divorce: Law and the Family in Canada.* Statistics Canada Cat. #89–502E (Ottawa: Minister of Supply and Services, 1983).
25 Ibid., p. 140.
26 Ibid.
27 See, for instance, the overview discussions in Diana E. H. Russell, *Sexual Exploitation: Rape, Child Sexual Abuse, and Workplace Harassment* (Beverly Hills, CA: Sage, 1984); and Julia R. and Herman Schwendiger, *Rape and Inequality* (Beverly Hills, CA: Sage, 1983). For wife battering in Canada, see Linda MacLeod, *Wife Battering in Canada: The Vicious Circle.* Canadian Advisory Council on the Status of Women (Ottawa: Minister of Supply and Services Canada, 1980).
28 McKie et al., *Divorce,* pp. 148–149.
29 Napoleon Chagnon, *Yanomamo: The Fierce People* (New York: Holt, Rinehart and Winston, 1977). This section is based on a paper written by Joanne Beaudoin, entitled "*Yanomamo: The Fierce People* – A Critical Analysis of Sexist Content" The paper was written for a seminar taught by M. Eichler at the Ontario Institute for Studies in Education. The student chose to criticize Chagnon's work because it was presented in another course as a good example of a case study in cultural anthropology.
30 Chagnon, *Yanomamo,* p. 83.
31 Economic Council of Canada, *On the Mend: Twentieth Annual Review* (Ottawa: Minister of Supply and Services, 1983).
32 Ibid., p. 89.
33 Ibid., Table A13, p. 118.
34 L. Alan Sroufe, Deborah Jacobvitz, Sarah Mangelsdorf, Edward DeAngelo, and

Mary Jo Ward, "Generational boundary dissolution between mothers and their preschool children: A relationship systems approach," *Child Development* 56, 2 (1985):317–325.

35 Ibid., p. 317.

36 Ibid., p. 318.

37 Ibid.

38 Ibid., p. 322.

39 Ibid., p. 320.

40 Ibid., p. 318.

41 Ibid., p. 319.

42 Ibid., p. 322.

43 Ibid., p. 323.

44 Judith Herman, *Father-Daughter Incest* (Cambridge, MA: Harvard University Press, 1981):42, as quoted in Russell, *Sexual Exploitation*, p. 264.

45 Russell, *Sexual Exploitation*, p. 264.

46 Mary Daly, *Gyn/Ecology: The Metaethics of Radical Feminism* (Boston: Beacon, 1978).

47 Daly, *Gyn/Ecology*, p. 116. In this passage, Daly cites P. Thomas, *Indian Women through the Ages* (New York: Asia Publishing, 1964): 263; this author describes the situation in Muslim India of widows who tried to escape cremation, writing that "to prevent her escape she was usually surrounded by men armed with sticks who goaded her on to her destination by physical force."

48 *Webster's* does not provide a date of publication. But I presume that I have a later edition as Daly's book appeared in 1978, and my edition lists Carter as U.S. president.

49 Paula J. Caplan, *The Myth of Women's Masochism* (New York: E. P. Dutton, 1985): 35–36.

50 Frank F. Furstenberg, Jr., "Sociological ventures in child development," *Child Development* 56, 2 (1985): 281–288, quote on p. 284.

51 Ibid.

52 For some of the reasons that researchers give to justify the exclusion of women from their research design, as well as consequences of such a practice, see Suzanne Prescott, "Why researchers don't study women: The responses of 62 researchers," *Sex Roles* 4, 6 (1978): 899–905.

53 Carol Gilligan, *In a Different Voice: Psychological Theory and Women's Development* (Cambridge, MA: Harvard University Press, 1982), p. 18. There has been considerable debate about Gilligan's own work, which, at times, exhibits the problem of sexual dichotomism.

54 Robert F. Bales and Philip E. Slater, "Role differentiation in small decision-making groups," in Talcott Parsons and Robert F. Bales (eds.), *Family, Socialization and Interaction Process* (Glencoe, IL: Free Press, 1955): 259–306.

55 For a more far-reaching critique, see Margrit Eichler, *The Double Standard* (London: Croom Helm, 1980):39–48.

56 These are items from the Brogan and Kutner inventory; see D. Brogan and N. G. Kutner, "Measuring sex-role orientation: A normative approach," *Journal of Marriage and the Family* 37 (1975): 391–399, but are here quoted from Kenrick S. Thompson, "Sex role orientation: A primer of scale construction," *International Journal of Sociology of the Family* 14, 1 (1984).

Chapter 3
Overgeneralization

3.1 Introduction

Overgeneralization may occur in the identification of a research project, in the language employed, in the concepts used, in the methods used, and in the interpretations made. It takes place each time a study deals with one sex only but presents itself as if it were of general (rather than sex-specific) applicability. This error is typically committed for both sexes, although in a sharply divergent

48

manner: men's experience tends to be seen as an appropriate basis for making general statements about practically anything but the family; women's experience tends to be seen as an appropriate basis for overgeneralization only about some aspects of family life or reproduction. The flip side of overgeneralization is overspecificity: a description of research that masks the true nature of the study.

3.2 Sexist Language

Sexist language tends to be defined as language that uses male terms for generic purposes, and indeed, this is the most frequent form of overgeneralization at the level of simple language. However, this definition is insufficient. Language is sexist whenever it uses (a) sex-specific terms for generic purposes (overgeneralization); or (b) generic terms for sex-specific purposes (overspecificity). In addition, language is sexist when it uses nonparallel terms for parallel situations, but this is a form of sexism that falls under the rubric of double standards and will be considered in more detail in Chapter 5.

3.2.1 Use of Sex-Specific Terms for Generic Purposes

The journals that were examined for sexism contained numerous instances of male terms used in a supposedly generic manner, but I did not find any female terms used in a supposedly generic manner.[1] (I *did* find the use of generic terms to refer to females only. See section 3.2.2.) We are here dealing with the time-honored practice of using "he," "man," or "mankind" as supposedly generic terms, and although some journals and some authors attempt to avoid this form of sexism, evidence of this practice can still be found.

So, for instance, institutions continue to be "manned" rather than staffed,[2] and "mankind" continues to be equated with humanity.[3] In other sources, we find that "man is a small group animal,"[4] and that the individual who joins an interest group is identified as "he," as is the individual who has some idea of what present and potential benefits are worth, or the person who is wooed by environmental lobbies.[5] In another article, the journalistic community is identified as the "journalistic fraternity," which, given the number of female journalists, is clearly inappropriate,[6] and the next door neighbor is also a "he":

> Imagine a friendly backyard conversation in which a governing member sets out to explain to his next-door neighbor why it is in everybody's interest to use part of the citizen's taxes to prevent him from receiving some kind of information about his world.[7]

Likewise, a sophisticated voter is presented as "he" in an article that analyzes Gallup Poll data that presumably are derived from female as well as male respondents.[8] Similarly, the "marginal individual, the one whose consumer surplus from entering the market is lowest" is also a "he."[9]

The examples cited above are not trivial. In a recent and highly acclaimed book on constructing questionnaires for survey research, the opening paragraph reads as follows:

> The central thesis of this book is that question wording is a crucial element in maximizing the validity of survey data obtained by a question-asking process. . . .
>
> The importance of the exact wording of the questions seems obvious and hardly worth dwelling on. The fact that seemingly small changes in wording can cause large differences in responses has been well known to survey practitioners since the early days of surveys.[10]

The authors then discuss how the word "you" can be either singular or plural and therefore tends to be a source of confusion. They suggest the use of "you, yourself," "you or any member of this household," or "you and all other members of this household" to ensure correct understanding of the meaning of a question.[11]

All of this is excellent advice, but the authors seem unaware that a similar confusion exists when dealing with supposedly generic words that are used for two purposes, that is, sometimes to indicate only males, and sometimes to mean both males and females. That this is not a simple oversight but is in fact not perceived by the authors becomes evident when one considers some of the sample questions that they supply. Although the book is otherwise most helpful, questions that use sexist language elicit no comment from the authors as being unspecific, inappropriate, ambiguous, or confusing. For instance, when providing a set of questions designed to measure attitudes toward freedom of speech, they provide the following examples without commenting on the language:

> There are always some people whose ideas are considered bad or dangerous by other people. For instance, somebody who is against all churches and religion . . .
>
>> A. If such a person wanted to make a speech in your city . . . against churches and religion, should he be allowed to speak, or not? . . .
>
> Or consider a person who believes that blacks are genetically inferior.
>
>> A. If such a person wanted to make a speech in your community claiming that blacks are inferior, should he be allowed to speak, or not? . . .
>
>> C. If some people in your community suggested that a book he wrote which said blacks are inferior should be taken out of your public library, would you favor removing this book, or not?
>
> Now, I should like to ask you some questions about a man who admits he is a Communist.
>
> Consider a person who advocated doing away with elections and letting the military run the country.
>
>> A. If such a person wanted to make a speech in your community, should he be allowed to speak, or not?[12]

These questions engender two different sets of problems, depending on how the responses are interpreted by the researcher. If the responses are taken to signify attitudes toward freedom of speech for all people, females as well as males, then clearly they are inappropriately phrased. It is quite possible that attitudes toward female, as opposed to male, homosexuals (another category of people identified later in this set of questions) would be quite different with respect to their right to speak, teach in a college or university, or have their book in a public library. The same might be true about attitudes toward male or female communists, promilitary people, racists, and so on. Extending results of this study to women without reformulation of the questions would be a serious overgeneralization.

On the other hand, if the questions were intended to identify people's attitudes toward freedom of speech for males only, this should have been made explicitly clear. For instance, the researcher might ask about a person and then specify "if a man ... " and "if a woman ... " were to do the following, should this be allowed or not? In this way, the referent would be absolutely clear.

3.2.2 Use of Generic Terms for Sex-Specific Purposes

This source of bias is caused by the use of generic terms to describe all-female or all-male groups. While I did not encounter a single example of a female term used for generic purposes (which does not mean that such terms do not exist), I did find a number of terms that sounded generic but which identified, in fact, only female or only male respondents. In the case of exclusively female referents, all of the examples I found dealt with some aspect of family or reproduction, while the use of generic terms as male referents covered a large range of areas.

We begin with an example of overgeneralization of female respondents. One frequently encountered generic term that is often employed to identify females only is "single parents." For instance, in a recent article entitled "Single Parents, Extended Households, and the Control of Adolescents," we find the following gross overgeneralization:

> Most of our analyses in this paper compare mother-only families with families containing both the biological father and the biological mother. ... Families containing step-parents are not included in our basic analyses. ... We also omit the few single-parent families headed by a father, thus providing a more homogeneous set of families for our comparisons. Essentially, family structure in this paper refers to

families in which the biological mother is always present and the biological father is either present or absent and not replaced by a step-father.[13]

Clearly, to identify this research as a study of single parents, given that only single mothers are considered (and that single fathers have deliberately been excluded), is highly inappropriate.

It is, however, not only the term "single parent" that is identified with mothers; the more general term "parent" is also often utilized inappropriately. For example, a study entitled "How Parents Label Objects for Young Children: The Role of Input in the Acquisition of Category Hierarchies" is, in fact, a study about how *mothers* teach concepts to their 2- to 4-year-old children, *not* about how mothers *and* fathers teach them.[14]

In the first few pages of this article, we read constantly about parents: "Parents use basic level terms much more than terms at other levels in their speech to children. ... Parents may discuss categories at different levels in ways to help children understand hierarchical organization. ... Parents often introduce basic level terms through ostensive definition. ... " and so on.[15] This use of the term "parents" continues until we come to a passage that reads:

A parent is not likely to point to an object and say, "This is a vehicle." She is much more likely to anchor at the basic level, saying, "This is a jeep; a jeep is a kind of vehicle."[16]

It is unclear whether the combination of "parent" and "she" means that the other studies cited also refer only to mothers. Since we know from other research that there are significant differences between male and female speech patterns, this would be a very important fact to establish.

When we come to the description of the author's own study, we learn that

in the two studies reported here, parents were asked to teach concepts at different levels to their 2- to 4-year-old children. In the first study, parents taught basic and superordinate concepts to their children. In the second study, another set of parents taught basic and subordinate concepts. The parents' teaching strategies were analyzed in terms of their potential usefulness for children who are attempting to learn about principles of hierarchical classification. . . . [17]

It is only when we come to the description of the methods used in these two studies that we learn that the subjects in the first study were fourteen mother-child pairs, and in the second study, sixteen mother-child pairs.[18] We also learned in a footnote that

> although all requests for subjects were addressed to "parents", virtually all of the respondents were mothers. One father did volunteer, but his son refused to cooperate, and thus could not be included in the study.[19]

A similar problem is encountered with the use of the terms "fertility" or "childlessness." For example, a recent article entitled "Childlessness in Canada 1971: A Further Analysis" examines correlates of childlessness in younger and older cohorts of ever-married (that is, married, widowed, divorced, or separated) women.[20] The article overgeneralizes in that it ignores mothers who have never been married (an overgeneralization, but not a sexist one) and male fertility altogether (a sexist overgeneralization). Although this is common practice among demographers, it is sexist nonetheless to equate childlessness with female childlessness. It leaves us ignorant about male childlessness and, in this case, ignorant of half of the phenomenon purportedly under study: Husbands of wives who are childless may not be childless themselves; conversely, husbands of wives with children may never have had a biological child themselves.

Examples of the use of generic terms for male-sex-specific studies or behaviors abound. Rather than belabor the point about overgeneral language, I will provide examples of the use of generic terms for males only in later sections as we consider identification of projects, research methods, and data interpretation. It is important to note, however, the overlap between overgeneral language and an androcentric perspective that is found in the use of generic terms for male-specific studies or behaviors. One reinforces the other.

3.3 Overgeneral Titles

In the previous section, we encountered several overgeneral titles (for example, childlessness in Canada turned out to be female childlessness; parents who label objects for young children turned out to be mothers; and single parents who control adolescents [or fail to] turned out to be exclusively mothers). All of the articles to be considered in the following sections also have overgeneral titles. For instance, an article entitled "The Elderly Sick Role: An Experimental Analysis" deals with the male sick role only.[21] Similarly, an article entitled "Ability Grouping and Contextual Determinants of Educational Expectations in Israel" deals with male students only.[22] Likewise, an article entitled "Number of Siblings and Educational Mobility" deals with male mobility only.[23]

The latter article is interesting in that the context of the article itself is *not* overgeneral. The article examines the impact of the father's education on his son's schooling and finds that this influence is conditional on "sibsize" (the number of sisters and brothers). The article does identify itself as a study of male mobility, not social mobility in general, and, indeed, we remain ignorant of the influence of sibsize or mother's education on women's educational mobility. Had the article been entitled "Number of Siblings and Educational Mobility from Father to Son," overgeneralization would not be a problem here.

The formulation of accurate titles (and other means of identifying research, such as key words, abstracts, and the like) is an important step in reducing sexism in research. If all the male-oriented studies were to state explicitly in their titles that they apply to males only, a significant amount of existing social science research would be properly identified, and the problem of imbalance of knowledge concerning males and females would become visible. Likewise, if the titles of female-specific studies relating to family and reproductive issues were not overgeneralized, a similar imbalance would also become visible. Making imbalances visible is not a solution to the overriding problem of selective attention, but it is certainly an important first step. "Truth in labeling" could result not only in less overgeneralization in interpretation and method, but also, one would hope, ultimately in more inclusive research.

3.4 Overgeneral Concepts

Just as language and titles can be overgeneral, so too can a concept itself be overgeneral, beyond the level of simple language. In order to recognize whether a concept overgeneralizes, we need to identify (a) the purported referent and (b) the empirical referent within the concept. When the purported referent is general while the empirical concept is sex-specific, we are dealing with an instance of overgeneralization. For example, in the concept of "universal suffrage" as applied to the French Revolution, the purported referent is all people, since the concept uses the term "universal." In fact, the empirical referents were male only, since women did not win the vote at that time.[24] The purported referents and the empirical referents do not match; hence we are dealing with an instance of overgeneralization. Similarly, the concepts of "child-lessness" or "fertility," when they are used to cover female childlessness and fertility only, are examples of the same problem.

An example of overspecificity in a concept can be found in the title of a recent article on "Nativity, Intermarriage, and Mother-Tongue Shift."[25] The term "mother-tongue" is overspecific since it refers not necessarily to the mother's tongue, but to the language a child first learns at home: it may be his or her mother's tongue, father's tongue, or a third language altogether. Although the author states that children are "probably more likely to speak their mother's first language ... than their father's first language,"[26] the concept remains inexact and could be replaced by mother's tongue, father's tongue, or parental tongue (when the same language is shared by both parents).[27]

3.5 Overgeneral Methods

Overgeneralization in methods can occur through inappropriate wording of questions (if questions are asked of respondents) and through underspecificity in reporting on the methods employed.

3.5.1 Inappropriate Wording of Questions

In the section on the use of sex-specific terms for generic purposes (3.2.1), we looked at one example of the wording of questions intended to measure freedom of speech. (These questions were taken from NORC General Social Surveys). A recent article on urbanism and tolerance[28] used a data set based on these questions "because they provide the most recent data using identical wordings for items tapping tolerance."[29] These questions ask about attitudes toward "people whose ideas are considered bad or dangerous by other people," such as "somebody who is against all churches and religions," "a person who believes that blacks are genetically inferior," "a man who admits he is a Communist," "a person who advocates doing away with elections and letting the military run the country," and "a man who admits that he is homosexual."

The author identifies this set of questions as "items [that] tap respondents' willingness to allow expression of various ideas rather than support for the ideas or the persons holding them."[30] Fair enough, but since the context of the questions makes it clear that "the persons holding such ideas" are males, an important dimension of the concept of tolerance is lost. Either this loss must be acknowledged, in which case the title as well as the discussion must specify that this is an article examining tolerance toward *males* who hold certain ideas, or women need to be included in the wording of the questions. This could be done by identifying the "person" as "he or she"; or by asking questions about women and men; or by creating two questionnaires, one that referred to women and one that referred to men, and using a split sample. The latter two techniques would allow for an analysis of whether respondents are more tolerant toward women or men who express various ideas, or whether there is no such difference.

3.5.2 Overspecificity in Reporting on the Methods Employed

Another problem one encounters from time to time is overspecificity in the reporting on methods employed. Other related methodological problems will be considered in the chapter on gender insensitivity.

In a recent article that employs secondary data analysis on citizen contacting in seven countries,[31] the authors use a data set from a seven-nation study by Verba, Nie, and Kim. Examples of citizen contactors are described as follows:

> unemployed workers looking for jobs, veterans with questions about military benefits, social security recipients in search of lost checks, builders seeking government contracts, and property owners angling for tax abatements are obvious instances. In developing nations, the list of contactors would also include peasants looking for access to markets, new city dwellers trying to adjust to their new living environment, and parents trying to keep their sons out of the army or looking for recommendations to help their children into universities.[32]

This list of examples might well include women. Women may be unemployed and looking for jobs, they may be social security recipients in search of lost checks, and so on. However, as one reads further, the description becomes unclear. The authors state that

> the approaches drawing on social and economic variables take no account of whether the person considering contacting believes it likely that he will succeed in affecting the political influential or whether the potential contactor has personal incentives or political obligations to help others.[33]

We then find a hypothesis that states that

> the greater the number and strength of political ties and obligations that a person has, the more likely he is to approach a government official to help himself or others. . . . [34]

and we learn that

> the variables are derived from answers to survey questions about whether or not the respondent has contacted local or extralocal

government officials or other powerful persons for help in addressing the needs of respondent, his family, friends, neighborhood, workmates, community or other social group, during the preceding two years. Particularized contacting combines local and extralocal efforts to help the contactor and his family.[35]

At this point, confusion reigns. Are female respondents included or are they not? The language suggests that they are excluded, but we cannot be sure.

On the same page, however, we stumble across a statement that suggests that indeed women were included, for we learn that individuals were ranked "by a combined measure of income and education that distinguishes sex levels on a cross-culturally equivalent scale."[36] Surely, this must mean that male and female contactors were included in the sample – possibly even some of the contactees were female? This impression is shattered by the last sentences of the article:

The party and campaign activist is the focal point for the contacting efforts of the people around him. Because he has the political connections and the political obligations, they turn to him for political assistance. This connection becomes the structural basis of the political ties that account for much of the social contacting that exists throughout the world.[37]

If, then, women were included, the language is highly inappropriate, and the reporting on the methods employed is overspecific. Given that there are significant differences in male and female political participation, it would furthermore have been theoretically important to do an analysis by sex and to test the various variables while taking sex into account. For instance, do education and political activism have the same effect on women's likelihood of contacting as they do on men's? This is a problem of gender insensitivity and will be discussed in Chapter 4. Finally, the way in which women are ranked in terms of income and education introduces an androcentric bias as discussed in Chapter 2.

3.6 Overgeneral Data Interpretation

When language and methods are overgeneral, it is almost inevitable that data interpretation will also overgeneralize. We will here consider only two recent examples of this problem.

First, a recent article on the elderly sick role[38] reports on a small experiment in which 126 undergraduate students responded to a vignette that was experimentally manipulated. It read as follows (manipulated variables in brackets);

> Mr. A. is [forty-eight years old, seventy-eight years old]. He is a widower, and has a daughter who lives about a mile from his home. He is a veteran, and now [works as a tailor, is retired]. Recently he has complained of back trouble which he says is painful and which interferes with his normal activities.[39]

Respondents were then asked "if this man or a member of his family should ask you for advice on some of the following matters, how would you respond?"

The design is clearly oriented toward one sex: a man who is supposed to represent "the elderly." Notwithstanding this clear sex identification, the title, the discussion, the data interpretation, and the conclusions are all couched in general terms. This is evident in the following excerpts from the results and discussion sections:

> The failure to achieve any significant effects by age for the expectations of role exemption and physician utilization argues against the existence of an ascribed elderly sick role along these dimensions of the Parsonian model. . . . Not depending on others or expressing need is a basic element of the socialization experience of our respondents. . . . There is some evidence that younger people, both lay and professional, may be hesitant to put the aged in dependent roles . . . the tendency for respondents not to expect the elderly to recover can be viewed as having a basis in reality. . . . However, from a sociological point of view the ascription of a terminal sick role to the elderly is a result of stereotyping.[40]

It is particularly ironic that in a study of the sick role of the elderly the referent is male, given that there are more elderly females than males and that the sick roles of females and males are defined quite differently. To make this article nonsexist, then, either the sex of the referent individual would also have to be manipulated and the data analyzed accordingly, or the identification of the study, its data interpretation, and its conclusions would have to be restricted to the *male* elderly sick role.

Our second example comes from the education literature. The title of the article, "Ability Grouping and Contextual Determinants of Educational Expectations in Israel,"[41] suggests that this is a general article on educational expectations in Israel. In fact, this is a study of "all male Jewish students who attended eighth grade in the national Religious and National school systems during 1968/69. The sample consists of 21,289 students, who attended 957 schools."[42] Footnote 1 informs us that "since that study [the Judas Matras's Life History Study of Jewish Men] concerns men only, data were not retrieved for females or non-Jewish students. Recently, a similar Life History study of women was completed. However, the Seker files for women are not yet available."[43]

Neither the introduction to the study, nor its discussion, nor its conclusion make us aware of the fact that this is a one-sex study. The introduction states:

This paper concerns the determinants of educational expectations among Israeli primary school students. We focus on the effects of school contexts on expectations and on the way these are conditioned by ability *grouping*. Previous research reveals small contextual effects on educational outcomes and tends to dismiss their importance in the educational attainment process.

In the present study, we compare the magnitude of contextual effects on expectations in a population of contextually heterogeneous schools, some of which practice ability grouping and some of which do not. The essence of our argument is that among dissimilar schools contextual effects can be large. However, where students are grouped, contextual school effects on expectations are eliminated and are replaced, in part, by group effects.[44]

The article continues in this vein. The conclusions are also grossly overgeneral, given that only the male half of the Israeli student population was considered. Nor do we learn whether the schools were coeducational or had only male students. Since one of the crucial variables is homegeneity versus heterogeneity, this might be of special significance when discussing ability grouping. Since girls were seen as heterogeneous enough to be excluded from the study, their participation or lack of it in ability groups might at least have been mentioned.

The discussion of the results begins as follows:

> To summarize, we have shown that where schools are highly variable in student-body composition they can exert strong contextual effects on grades and educational expectations. In ungrouped Israeli schools the effects of contextual aptitude and socioeconomic status on grades are negative and serve to attenuate inequality between ethnic and socioeconomic groups. Contextual effects on educational expectations are also large, but they operate in opposite directions and offset one another.[45]

The interpretation of the data, therefore, suffers from severe overgeneralization due to the fact that girls are not considered and that this fact is not taken into account in the body of the text. It is also, one suspects, a reflection of an androcentric bias, since if this article were based on girls only, one could expect it to be entitled "Ability Grouping and Contextual Determinants of Educational Expectations for Girls in Israel."

3.7 Conclusion

Unlike identifying androcentricity in research, identifying – and rectifying – overgeneralizations or instances of overspecificity is a relatively straightforward and comparatively simple matter. While appropriate identification in language, concepts, methods, and data interpretation would not rectify all aspects of sexism in research (e.g., a lopsided attention to certain issues), it would make such phenomena more visible, thus facilitating their eventual correction.

Notes

1 The one term that might be considered an exception is "mother tongue," but since this term is used to deal with cases of "mother tongue," "father tongue," and "parent tongue," the problem is one of overspecificity rather than overgeneralization. See section 3.4.

2 R. Paul Shaw, "Humanity's propensity for warfare: A Sociobiological perspective," *Canadian Revue of Sociology and Anthropology* 22, 2 (1985): 227–232, quote p. 173.

3 Ibid., p. 176.

4 Roger Krohn, "Is sociobiology a political or research program?" *Canadian Review of Sociology and Anthropology* 22, 2 (1985): 227–232, quote p. 229.

5 John Mark Hansen, "The political economy of group membership," *American Political Science Review* 79, 1 (1985): 79–96, quoted on pp. 80 and 81.

6 Philip E. Converse, "Power and the monopoly of information," APSA Presidential Address, 1984, *American Political Science Review* 79, 1 (1985): 1–9, quote p. 2.

7 Ibid.

8 Henry W. Chappell, Jr., and William R. Keech, "A new view of political accountability for economic performance," *American Political Science Review* 79, 1 (1985): 10–27; see, e.g., pp. 13 and 15.

9 Joseph E. Stiglitz, "Information and economic analysis: A perspective," *Supplement to the Economic Journal* 95 (1985): 25.

10 Seymour Sudman and Norman M. Bradburn, *Asking Questions: A Practical Guide to Questionnaire Design* (San Francisco:Jossey-Bass, 1982):1.

11 Ibid., p. 40.

12 Ibid., pp. 129–131.

13 Sanford M. Dornbush et al., "Single parents, extended households, and the control of adolescents," *Child Development* 56, 2 (1985): 326–341, quote p. 328.

14 Maureen A. Callanan, "How parents label objects for young children: The role of input in the acquisition of category hierarchies," *Child Development* 56, 2 (1985): 508–523.

15 Ibid., pp. 508–509.

16 Ibid., p. 510.

17 Ibid.

18 Ibid., pp. 510, 516.

19 Ibid.,p. 510,fn. 1.

20 Nigel Tomes, "Childlessness in Canada 1971: A further analysis," *Canadian Journal of Sociology* 10, 1 (1985): pp. 37–68.

21 William Fisher, Arnold Arluke, and Jack Levin, "The elderly sick role: An experimental analysis," *International Journal of Aging and Human Development* 20,3(1984–85):161–164.

22 Yossi Shavit and Richard A. Williams, "Ability grouping and contextual determinants of educational expectations in Israel," *American Sociological Review* 50, 1 (1985): 62–73.

23 Judith Blake, "Number of siblings and educational mobility," *American Sociological Review* 50, 1 (1985): 84–95.

24 In fact, the term did not refer even to all males as class and race were hidden distinctions as well.

25 Gillian Stevens, "Nativity, intermarriage, and mother-tongue shift," *American Sociological Review* 50, 1 (1985): 74–83.
26 Ibid., p. 77.
27 This particular study dealt with children, about 10 percent of whom were "children of linguistically heterogamous marriages"; ibid., p. 78, fn. 3.
28 Thomas C. Wilson, "Urbanism and tolerance: A test of some hypotheses drawn from Wirth and Stouffer," *American Sociological Review* 50, 1 (1985): 117–123.
29 Ibid., p. 119, fn. 1.
30 Ibid.
31 Alan S. Zuckerman and Darrell M. West, "The political bases of citizen contacting: A cross-national analysis," *American Political Science Review* 79, 1 (1985): 117–131.
32 Ibid., p. 117.
33 Ibid., p. 119.
34 Ibid.
35 Ibid., p. 122.
36 Ibid.
37 Ibid., p. 131.
38 Fisher, Arluke, and Levin, "The elderly sick role," pp. 161–165.
39 Ibid., p. 163.
40 Ibid., p. 164.
41 Shavit and Williams, "Ability Grouping," pp. 62–73.
42 Ibid., p. 64–65.
43 Ibid.
44 Ibid., p. 62.
45 Ibid., p. 70.

Chapter 4
Gender Insensitivity

4.1 Introduction

Gender insensitivity, our third primary sexist problem, is in many ways the simplest one. It appears in only one form, rather than in multiple forms, as we found with androcentricity and overgeneralization. It quite simply consists of ignoring sex as an important social variable.

Such gender insensitivity may or may not be an outgrowth of an androcentric bias. In most cases, it will be difficult or impossible to tell, because typically in a piece of work that is gender insensitive, the reader is not given sufficient information to determine, for instance, the sex of participants in the research process; it is simply regarded as too unimportant to mention.

4.2 *Ignoring Sex as a Socially Significant Variable*

While sifting through the various journals that provide the bulk of examples for this book, I found an entire issue of the *American Journal of Psychology* in which every single article is blind to sex as an important social variable. Of the seven substantive articles in that issue, one might potentially argue that for one of the articles,[1] sex is not an important variable (the article attempts to quantify beauty in an abstract sense). On the other hand, confirmation of any hypothesis about beauty depends on experiments in which subjects rate the beauty of various figures; one can therefore legitimately ask whether sex plays a role in determining aesthetic pleasure. The literature that is reported is not discussed in terms of a sex effect. This may either mean that the studies reported are also gender insensitive, or it may mean that these particular authors have ignored any reference to gender in their use of previously published material.

All of the other articles in this issue involve experimental subjects. One article[2] examines subjects' ability to recall prose passages read to them. The subjects are described as "104 college students who participated in the experiment as part of a course requirement. Half were enrolled in educational psychology courses at the University of Illinois, and half were enrolled in psychology courses at Millkin University."[3] No mention of the sex of the respondents is made. Given that there are observed differences in verbal ability between the sexes, one wonders why it is more important to identify the students' university affiliations than their sex. Presumably they were both female and male – but who knows?

The next article[4] examines learning of a perceptually isolated or prelearned item in a continuous series. Three experiments are reported. Subjects of the first experiment are identified as "96 student volunteers from sections of the introductory psychology course at Western Washington University. Participation was encouraged as part of a course requirement." Subjects in the second experiment were presumably the same, since "Experiment 2 was in keeping with the design of Experiment 1 except that prelearning one of the trigrams was substituted for perceptual isolation. . . . All other methodological features matched those described for Experiment 1."[5] The write-up suggests that the subjects in Experiment 3 were probably the same students as well.[6] At no point is there any discussion of the respondents' sex.

The next article[7] investigates the relative preferences of rhesus monkeys for reward probability versus amount. Subjects are identified as "8 rhesus monkeys . . . with test experience. There were 4 males and 4 females, between 4 and 6 years of age." Experimental groups were structured to have equal female and male participation, but the results are not analyzed (or discussed) in terms of the sex of the subjects. While the research design is not gender insensitive, the data interpretation is.

Another article[8] examines how stimulus probability affects encoding. Two experiments are described. Subjects of the first experiment are identified as "24 right-handed members of the University of Michigan paid-subject pool."[9] Participants in the second experiment are described as "36 right-handed members of the University of Michigan paid-subject pool."[10] Since the sex of the subjects is not identified, it is clear that no analysis by sex was made.

A subsequent article[11] describes three experiments investigating the differences between two types of spatial location memory: memory for the location of individual items in an array, and memory for occupied, as opposed to unoccupied, locations in an array. Experiment 1 examined the memory of elderly adults and young college students. Participants are described as follows:

> Participating in Experiment 1 were 52 persons, 24 community-dwelling elderly individuals (mean age = 69.4 years, range = 60–80 years) and 28 undergraduate psychology students at the University of North Carolina at Charlotte (UNCC) (mean age = 21.2 years, range = 17–30 years). College students were given course credit for participating. The older group was made up of volunteers recruited from the "Charlotte Senior Scholars" organization and from UNCC's summer "Elderhostel" program.[12]

Experiment 2 was undertaken to replicate the findings of Experiment 1 and to compare item location memory and occupied location memory for objects and matched words. Subjects are described as follows:

> Participating in Experiment 2 were 96 persons: 48 community-dwelling elderly individuals (mean age = 68.2 years, range = 59–80 years) and 48 students from the University of North Carolina at Charlotte (mean age = 19.0 years, range = 17–25 years). Elderly individuals were obtained in response to a newspaper story indicating the need for participants. All subjects were paid for their participation.[13]

Experiment 3 examined memory for occupied locations independent of item location and location memory. Participants in this last experiment were described as follows:

> Because the analyses of Experiments 1 and 2 evinced no interactions of age and memory for occupied locations, only college students were tested in Experiment 3. Participants were 48 undergraduates (mean age = 20.4 years, range 17–24 years) from the University of North Carolina at Charlotte. Subjects were either paid or given course credit for participation.

The study concludes that

> spatial memory is not a simple, global process. Different components of spatial memory may be affected differently by variations in stimulus characteristics or experimental design, and these components may or may not interact with each other depending upon the demands of specific tasks."[14]

It seems reasonable to ask whether the sex of the person remembering has any effect on the memory, particularly given the fact that differences in spatial–visual abilities are one of the few consistently documented sex differences.[15] Since the data are not analyzed by sex (assuming that both sexes participated, as seems likely), the question remains unanswered. The final article[16] exhibits the same pattern as the preceding ones. Six experiments are described, and in each case, the identification of subjects is sketchy and inconsistent, but always gender insensitive.

Looking at these articles as a group, and knowing full well that such articles are usually written in isolation from one another (but are nevertheless indicative of the editorial policy of the journal), we can see that the subjects are described generally in an extremely poor, nonstandardized manner, ranging from simple numbers ("46 observers") to identification of *how* they were chosen, whether or not they were paid, which university or organization they belonged to, their age, whether they were right-handed or not, whether they had participated in a previous experiment or not, and so on. In the case of the article on the rhesus monkeys, the sex of the subjects was identified, but in the six articles dealing with humans, not a single one specified the sex of its subjects. One is thus inclined to assume that sex may be of some importance when studying monkeys (but not enough to warrant an analysis), while for the study of humans, sex is not important (in fact, it is considered so irrelevant that it is not even mentioned).

One should not suppose that only psychology can be gender insensitive; in fact, such insensitivity can be found in all of the social sciences. Linda Christiansen-Ruffman has reported in a study of articles on participation in voluntary organizations that in

all volumes (1972–1983) of the *Journal of Voluntary Action Research* ... the vast majority of articles have ignored gender almost totally. In 232 of the 260 articles or 89%, sex or gender was neither a prime nor secondary analytic focus.[17]

In spite of the relative ease in collecting data on sex or gender, only 11% included this variable as part of analysis, and the variable received only very minimal attention in a number of the 17 cases in which gender was treated as one of the secondary foci. This lack of attention is not unique to this particular journal. In examining the participation literature contained in the Abstracts of the Association for Voluntary Action Scholars for the first three issues and for the most recent issue, the percentages were even lower than the Journal in terms of a focus on women.[18]

After examining all of the articles that focus on sex and/or gender (whether this was mentioned in the title or not) and all articles devoted to women, the author concludes:

> Thus women are not only relatively invisible, but theories of participation are not applicable in some of the few times when research is reported. ... The confusion and ambiguity in language (does "he" refer to a male person or to any person) reflects and is symptomatic of an analytic confusion.[19]

As a final example of the confusion and inaccuracy of gender-insensitive research, we shall consider a study of out-migration and subsequent return migration from and to Newfoundland.[20] This study reports on a survey of Newfoundland returnees (55 percent male, 47 percent female) and on additional data collected in the Bay of Islands in 1981 and 1982. At some point it is noted that "66 persons" were interviewed,[21] so presumably this constitutes the sample mentioned later.[22] We learn that, according to another survey, "63 percent of males and 55 percent of females had emigrated. In turn, 62 percent of migrant males and 48 percent of females returned."[23] This is a significant difference in return rates. It would have been most interesting to learn how many of the 66 "persons" were males and females, but we are not given this information. Instead, we find some tables that identify the occupational status of returned migrants (a table that does not include the category "housewife"), as well as another table that lists reasons for leaving Newfoundland. In this table, "family matters" are listed as reasons in only 5.5 percent of the cases, which suggests that perhaps all the "persons" were men? In any case, there is no breakdown by sex in the tables and none that can be reconstructed from the text. For example, we learn that the savings migrants brought with them "tend to be modest."[24] Given earning differentials between women and men, one would assume that there would be a significant difference in amounts saved by men and by women, but there is no way to determine this.

There is also a table on motivation for return migration, which lists as reasons "household head unemployed" and "household head didn't like job."[25] It remains unclear who is a household head.

The unemployed male? The female if she is not married? The employed female? A passage preceding this particular table only compounds the confusion:

> Half of surveyed household heads reported unemployment at some time of each year since returning, and nearly 30 percent were unemployed at the time of the 1979 survey. (An equivalent percentage of respondents' spouses were also unemployed at this time.)[26]

Although we do not know the sex composition of the sample, we can be reasonably sure that it includes men (or consists entirely of men); if it included only women, the sample would have been characterized as female. At least some – possibly all – household heads were married (they had spouses according to the preceding quotation); one can assume that they were male, since the usual practice is to define the male as the head of household and the wife as the spouse, rather than the other way around. However, this distinction remains unclear, and the information that can be gleaned from this article is thus, like the migrants' savings, very modest.

4.3 Failing to Analyze Sex-Differentiated Data by Sex

Sometimes, data are collected on both sexes but the analysis fails to take sex into account. One example is a study that examines the relationship among coping resources, life changes, and negative changes in health among the elderly.[27] The sample on which this study is based consisted of 132 males and 167 females. Coping resources examined were: self-efficacy, religiosity, social resources, marital status, occupational status, and income. The results are described as follows:

> The results of the present study suggest that of the several variables often cited in the literature as coping resources, only one of them,

income, seems to serve this function for the elderly. Social resources, religiosity, marriage, and the presence of a confidant were not significantly related to illness, either as a main effect or in interaction with life change. And, although feelings of self-efficacy and occupational status both showed significant salutory main effects, during times of high life change they appear to be coping inhibitors. For the elderly, it seems that possessing these characteristics serves to impede rather than facilitate an effective coping response.[28]

In speculating on the meaning of these findings, the authors offer several hypotheses, such as the following, to explain the failure of high occupational status to function as a coping resource:

One might speculate that the latter finding is a function of the fact that high status persons suffer greater loss of ego in the face of the unavoidable and potentially humiliating life events that accompany old age (e.g., retirement, physical impairment, moving to a care facility). The life changes in old age are, in a sense, powerful status levellers. . . . Any such status leveling or shifting to new status criteria would involve more loss for individuals of high occupational status than for those of low occupational status.[29]

Had the data been analyzed separately by sex of respondent, it is conceivable that the pattern found would have been different, since men tend to have higher-status occupations (and thus presumably will experience greater leveling) than women. Until the data are analyzed by sex, we cannot place much confidence in these conclusions. Similarly, the fact that marital status had no effect as a coping resource could mean that it truly is not a coping resource for either women or men; it could also mean that it has a negative effect on one sex and a positive effect on the other, effects that cancel each other out when the analysis is done on both sexes together. This latter hypothesis is suggested by the fairly consistent findings that marriage tends to place greater demands on women than on men. In addition, given that men tend to marry women who are younger than themselves, and that women live, on average, longer than men, it is reasonable to assume that many of the married women had to care for their husbands (who were older than they were), while few of the men would have had to care in the same manner for their wives.

Neglect of sex as an analytic variable, like other sexist research practices, can be found in all areas of the social sciences. In political science, we find a similar example: Sidney Verba and Norman Nie's study of political participation in America.[30] In this study, Verba and Nie developed six measures of participation in order to score a variety of groups for "over-" or "under-" representation in political participation. The total extent of Verba and Nie's discussion of female–male differences in participation is the conclusion that "men are somewhat over-represented in the most activist political groups but not to a very great degree."[31] However, as Judith Hicks Stiehm notes in her critique of Verba and Nie's work, the authors do find differences in the participation of blacks and whites "to be both important and interesting."

> A full chapter is devoted to their analysis. But what did the data show? What did the table look like which produced these conclusions? Black-white differences on the six measures varied from 4–27%. There was a 15% average difference. Female-male differences ranged from 11 to 28% with a 19% average difference. Female-male differences were clearly greater than black-white yet the female-male data were essentially disregarded while the black-white data were carefully discussed.[32]

Stiehm also notes that this volume won an American Political Science Association Award as the best new book in its field, and that it was especially commended for its methodology.[33] Gender insensitivity indeed!

Failing to analyze data by sex when they have been collected on both sexes may thus severely limit the utility of any findings and may, in fact, hide some of the most important aspects of a phenomenon. This would be true for all cases in which there is a significant social difference between the sexes. Because gender only rarely does *not* serve as a differentiating variable, the only safe course to take is to routinely analyze data by sex; if and only when it is shown empirically to be insignificant, collapse the data.[34]

Failing to do so can have not only serious theoretical consequences, but even more serious policy consequences as well. Constantina Safilios-Rothschild has documented this point in an overview article on women's invisibility in agriculture.[35] She notes that census statistics indicate that in most sub-Saharan countries, from two-fifths to over half of those economically active in agriculture are women, yet women's role in agriculture is nonetheless minimized.[36] Turning to Sierra Leone as a case study, she notes that

> the available statistics indicate that 45% of persons economically active in agriculture in 1970–71 were women, and research undertaken in different districts and chiefdoms suggests that most of these women were not unpaid family workers. Despite the very active role that women play in agriculture in Sierra Leone, international development agencies still view them primarily as unpaid farm labor responsible only for time-consuming and unskilled tasks such as weeding. Women farmers and women's active involvement in agriculture usually remain invisible because data on farmers are not disaggregated by sex in agricultural mission reports and feasibility studies.[37]

She then discusses an evaluation study that underlined the fact that women farmers are not only auxiliary farm workers but independent farmers in their own right, involved in the cultivation of cash crops – and not only in subsistence agriculture. Despite this fact, ongoing agricultural development programs are overwhelmingly directed to male farmers.

Here we are dealing not only with a problem of gender insensitivity, but also with androcentric bias, because the criteria used to determine eligibility for participation in the project are geared toward male and not female farmers. The problem is compounded by methodological bias: "The project did not keep information on the gender of the registered (or participating) farmers, and for this reason it was possible to believe that the project was reaching all farmers regardless of sex."[38] Being gender sensitive is certainly no guarantee of nonsexist policies, but it is a necessary precondition for assessing the degree of sexism in a given policy or project.

4.4 *Treating Other-Sex Opinions as Fact*

So far, we have looked at examples of gender insensitivity that are characterized primarily by failing to take sex into account. There is another, less obvious, form of gender insensitivity, in which a researcher asks members of one sex questions about both sexes and treats the answers as facts rather than opinions. While it is not wrong to ask males about their opinions of females and vice versa, it is wrong to treat answers about the other sex as if they were facts rather than opinions.

For example, in Chapter 2 (Androcentricity) we looked briefly at an ethnographic account of the Yanomamo, the "fierce people." We found that the study was conducted from a male viewpoint. The author, Chagnon, used two main informants to aid him in gathering his data. Not surprisingly, both were men. Given that the Yanomamo have a patriarchal, misogynist culture, there is a distinct possibility that Chagnon would not have been able to use women as informants had he wanted to do so. Likewise, a hypothetical female coresearcher might have been denied access to the village altogether. Practical problems in contacting women directly therefore surely existed. Nevertheless, the author should acknowledge the inevitable bias that derives from using male informants only. This acknowledgment is missing.

Instead, when discussing the subject of spousal infidelity, Chagnon describes his chief informant's marriage as follows: "She [the wife] and Kaobawa have a very tranquil household. He only beats her once in a while and never very hard. She never has affairs with other men."[39] Obviously (or so one would think), in an investigation of female infidelity in marriage, the husband is probably the least authoritative source. The only logical person to ask is the woman herself, especially when the penalty for female infidelity may be severe abuse and disfigurement. In this case, the wife might not have described their household as "very tranquil," since the family violence is directed at her. The source of information is also an important issue in historical research. All efforts should be made to gather information from a variety of sources. In those cases in which data are available from only one sex, this fact should be acknowledged and its implications explored.

Looking at another article already cited in Chapter 3 (Over-generalization), the study of single parents and the control of adolescents, we find that the interviewers asked the adolescent and one of the parents to answer independently four questions on decision making. The answers of the adolescent and the parent were then combined, as were answers that referred to the separate influence of the mother and the father, so that the parents are treated as a unit.[40]

This latter practice – conflating the mother's and father's opinions into a single "parental" attitude – is an example of familism, which will be discussed in Chapter 6. However, the practice of asking one spouse about the other seems to be sometimes acceptable within certain areas of investigation. For example, in family decision-making research, the woman will sometimes be asked who makes the decisions in her family: her husband, herself, or both of them.[41] This practice continues although we know that the responses of wives and husbands often differ considerably.[42] Compare this to asking respondents not only about their own voting behavior, but also about that of other household members. How much trust would we put in the accuracy of data generated in such a manner, beyond regarding them as perceptions that may or may not be in accord with reality?

4.5 Failing to Consider the Sex of All Participants in the Research Process

The two examples we have just looked at are really specialized instances of a more generalized problem: a failure to consider the sex of all the participants in the research process. These referred to informants in an ethnographic study and respondents in a social-psychological study. Depending on the type of study, there may be the following participants:

- the research subjects or respondents
- the researcher or research team
- the experimenter(s)

- experimenter(s)' confederate(s) in experimental research
- interviewers
- informants
- authors of statements (e.g., in historical research)
- sexually identified stimuli (e.g., cue cards that depict females and/or males in various situations, girl or boy dolls, animals identified as female or male, and so on)

We have already discussed the need to take the sex of research subjects, respondents, and informants into account. The sex of the researcher or of the members of the research team may also be important, depending on whether there is any direct interaction between the researcher and the subjects of the study. It is probably not important in statistical analyses, for example, assuming that other potential sources of sexism have been eliminated from the research process.

On the other hand, where researchers interact directly in some form with their respondents, the sex of the researchers may be important, depending on the subject under investigation. The same applies to interviewers. In some areas of investigation, it has been shown that the information obtained by male and female interviewers is comparable; in areas that are differentially sensitive for members of the two sexes (such as incest, abuse, battering, prostitution, sexual behaviors, infertility, male–female relations in general, and feminism), responses may vary with the sex of the interviewer. In all cases in which participant observation methods are employed, the sex of the researcher will be significant. While it will not always be possible to control for the sex of interviewers and researchers due to practical constraints, at a minimum the sex of the researcher-interviewer should be explicitly mentioned and possible effects should be considered.

Parallel comments apply to the role of experimenters or experimenters' confederates. It is a very well documented fact that subjects may respond differently according to the sex of experimenters and other participants in the research process.[43] In addition, there is evidence to show that experimenters behave differently toward subjects on the basis of their sex.

Because experimenters behave differently to male and female subjects even while administering the same formally approved procedures, male and female subjects may, psychologically, simply not be in the same experiment at all. In order to assess the extent to which obtained sex differences have been due to differential behavior toward male and female subjects, it would be necessary to compare sex differences obtained in those studies that depended for their data on a personal interaction with the subject and those that did not.[44]

Finally, the argument for identifying and controlling for sexually identified cues or stimuli in experiments is parallel to that for being sensitive to the gender of participants in the research process: it is simply a matter of accuracy and clarity to control for the sex of all visual, material, and other cues.

4.6 Decontextualization

So long as the social positions of males and females are significantly different, it will be necessary to recognize that a given situation may have very different meanings and implications for the members of each sex. For instance, marriage has very different implications and consequences for women than it does for men.[45] Likewise, divorce tends to be a very different experience for the female and the male involved in it.[46] Similar arguments have been made about political participation,[47] participation in education,[48] and the experience of particular residential locations.[49] Failing to ask whether a situation has different implications for females and males affected by it is another common form of gender insensitivity.

Let us consider the example of an alternative model to explain the emergence and development of nineteenth-century industrializ-ation.[50] Among other things, the authors note that

the central and defining experience of each new generation was automatic and collective induction into local industry. Young people in these regions seemed to absorb the knowledge required in production incidentally, as a natural part of growing up.

At the same time youngsters in these districts learned about products and production methods, they learned the rules of competition and whom they could trust to abide by them. ... This was as important for those who spent their working lives inside large firms as for those who went into business for themselves. For instance, at the same time as the "cellar lad" starting out in Sheffield steelworks imbibed knowledge about metallurgical materials and methods, he learned to appraise the character of his workmates and superiors.[51]

In the nineteenth century, there were also many girls and women working in various local industries. While at its beginning the quoted passage seems applicable to all workers, toward the end it takes on a distinctly male character: the "cellar lad ... he learned." However, the article continues to speak in general terms:

In a world where youngsters were often trained to study character as a condition of economic survival it was important to maintain a character that would bear scrutiny. ...

Thus the process of socialization created a community across and within generations that protected the economy as a whole against the consequences of short-term calculations of advantage. ...

But this experience of community went hand in hand with the expectation that exceptional talent and drive would be rewarded.[52]

It is likely that females could *not* expect that their exceptional talent and drive would be rewarded in the same manner in which males could. The authors thus ignore one entire dimension of the issue they are discussing by failing to ask about the situation of females versus that of males involved in industry in the nineteenth century. By ignoring this context, the authors fail to see that, although both males and females participated in industry, their experiences were likely to be sharply divergent.

In another example we find an example of gender insensitivity that overlaps with androcentricity. The question at issue is what causes observed male/female income disparity. The authors posit what they call the "marriage asymmetry hypothesis" against the "employer discrimination hypothesis." The former maintains that marriage enhances male and reduces female incomes, because of unequal child and house care responsibilities, and because the marriage partners act as a team, in effect raising total incomes, which are misleadingly assigned to the husband alone by our statisticians.[53]

This argument hinges on a comparison of the average annual earnings of full-time male and female married and unmarried workers. The authors find that the wage differential between unmarried male and female workers is much smaller than that between married male and female workers.

There are at least two problems with this analysis. First of all, the vast majority of women and men marry at some point. Since the analysis contrasts only never-married workers against all others (including those who have married but are then divorced or widowed), the authors have ruled out well over 90 percent of the relevant population as irrelevant, hardly a useful approach. More important, the men and the women who never marry during their entire lifetime constitute very different groups, as Jessie Bernard has pointed out:

> By and large, both men and women tend to marry mates with the same general class and cultural background; there is "homogamy." But within that common background, men tend to marry women slightly below them in such measurable items as age, education, and occupation, and, presumably, in other as yet unmeasurable items as well. The result is that there is no one for the men at the bottom to marry, no one to look up to them. Conversely, there is no one for the women at the top to look up to; there are no men who are superior to them.[54]

Thus she characterizes the never-married women as the "cream-of-the-crop" and the never-married men as the "bottom-of-the-barrel."

By ignoring the context of being unmarried, the study's conclusions about the effect of sex on wages are highly misleading. In addition, the researchers' findings in favor of the "marriage assymetry hypothesis" in effect deny that there is wage discrimination on the basis of sex, thereby protecting male interests. The study thus suffers from androcentric bias as well.

4.7 Sex-Blind Policy Evaluations and Proposals

A particularly important subform of contextual gender insensitivity emerges in studies that either concern policy directly or have policy implications. One example is provided by the recent report of the Royal Commission on the Economic Union and Development Prospects for Canada.[55] The Commission recommends, among other things, free trade between the United States and Canada. This would cause, among other things, the loss of jobs in the manufacturing and service sectors.[56] These losses would occur primarily in sectors that have high concentrations of female workers: textiles, clothing, small electrical products, sporting goods, toys and games, and leather products. Two-thirds of the workers in these six industries are women. Benefits from free trade are expected for urban transit and forestry products, sectors dominated by men.

The Commission does recommend substantial temporary adjust-ment policies to retrain and relocate displaced workers who are suitably adaptable. However, this requires that workers indicate a "willingness to undertake adaptive behaviour"; this usually translates into a readiness to relocate. For married women this is often a virtual impossibility, since most families live where employment is available to males simply because the males are better paid.

This report thus proposes a policy that promises to have disproportionately disadvantageous consequences for women, and it offers a remedy for these consequences that would be available only on a very restricted basis. A nonsexist approach would have recognized the differential effect and either not recommended this particular policy or else suggested compensatory policies that would be tailored to the needs of the sex most disadvantaged.

4.8 Conclusion

Gender insensitivity appears essentially in one form: ignoring sex as a socially important variable. This silence about sex often makes it impossible to determine whether other sexist problems (e.g., androcentricity or overgeneralization) are present as well. Because of this, overcoming gender insensitivity is an important precondition for identifying and correcting other forms of sexism in research. One derivative form of gender insensitivity, familism, is so important that it will be discussed in greater detail in Chapter 6.

Notes

1   Frank Boselie and Emanuel Leeuwenber, "Birkhoff revisited: Beauty as a function of effect and means," *American Journal of Psychology* 98, 1 (1985): 1–40.

2   Stephen G. Whilhite, "Differential effects of high-level and low-level postpassage questions," *American Journal of Psychology* 98, 1 (1985): 41–58.

3   Ibid., p. 43.

4   Louis G. Lipman, "Serial isolation and response production," *American Journal of Psychology* 98, 1 (1985): 59–76.

5   Ibid., p. 66.

6   Ibid., p. 71.

7   Charles W. Hill and Arthur J. Riopelle, "Probability-reward preferences of rhesus monkeys," *American Journal of Psychology* 98, 1 (1985): 77–84.

8   David E. Irwin and Robert G. Pachella, "Effects of stimulus probability and visual similarity on stimulus encoding," *American Journal of Psychology* 98, 1 (1985): 84–100.

9   Ibid., p. 87.

10   Ibid., p. 92.

11   Thomas J. Puglisi, Denise Cortis Park, Anderson D. Smith, and Gregory W. Hill, "Memory for two types of spatial location: Effects of instruments, age and format," *American Journal of Psychology* 98, 1 (1985): 101–118.

12   Ibid., p. 104.

13   Ibid., p. 108.

14   Ibid., p. 115.

15   This belief may be ill-founded, however. New research has questioned whether sex-related differences in spatial abilities actually do exist; see Paula J. Caplan, Gael M. Macpherson, and Patricia Tobin, "Do sex-related differences in spatial abilities exist? A multilevel critique with new data," *American Psychologist* 40, 7 (1985): 786–799.

16   Jose Aparecida Da Silva, "Scales for perceived egocentric distance in a large open field: Comparison of three psychophysical methods," *American Journal of Psychology* 98, 1 (1985): 119–144.

17   Linda Christiansen-Ruffman, "Participation theory and the methodological construction of invisible women: Feminism's call for appropriate methodology," *Journal of Voluntary Action Research* 14, 2–3 (1985): 96.

18   Ibid., fn. 6, p. 107.

19   Ibid., p. 96–97.

20 Barnett Richling, "'You'd never starve here': Return migration to rural Newfound-land," *Canadian Review of Sociology and Anthropology* 22, 2 (1985):236–249.

21 Ibid., p. 238.

22 Ibid., p. 243.

23 Ibid., p. 237.

24 Ibid., p. 245.

25 Ibid., p. 244.

26 Ibid., p. 237.

27 Ronald L. Simons and Gale E. West, "Life changes, coping resources, and health among the elderly," *International Journal of Aging and Human Development* 20, 3 (1984–85): 173–189.

28 Ibid., p. 183.

29 Ibid.

30 Sidney Verba and Norman Nie, *Participation in America* (New York: Harper & Row, 1972). This is not as recent an example as the others cited but is included because of the important place this study occupies in American political science.

31 Verba and Nie, *Participation*, pp. 98–101.

32 Judith Hicks Stiehm, "The unit of political analysis: Our Aristotelian hangover," in Sandra Harding and Merrill B. Hintikka (eds.), *Discovering Reality: Feminist Perspectives on Epistemology, Metaphysics, Methodology, and Philosophy of Science* (Dordrecht: D. Reidel, 1983): 31–44; quote from p. 33.

33 Ibid., p. 32.

34 It should be noted that a finding of sex similarity often is significant in its own right.

35 Constantina Safilios-Rothschild, "The persistence of women's invisibility in agriculture: Theoretical and policy lessons from Lesotho and Sierra Leone," *Economic Development and Cultural Change* 33, 2 (1985):299–317.

36 Ibid., p. 300.

37 Ibid., p. 307.

38 Ibid., p. 308.

39 Napoleon Chagnon, *Yanomamo: The Fierce People* (New York: Holt, Rinehart and Winston, 1977): 15. This section is based on Beaudoin's paper (see Chapter 2, note 33).

40 Sanford M. Dornbusch et al., "Single parents, extended households, and the control of adolescents," *Child Development* 56, 2 (1985): 326–341.

41 For example, see Joyce E. Elliott and William Moskoff, "Decision-making power in Romanian families," *Journal of Comparative Family Studies* 14, 1 (1983): 39–50.

42 See Craig M. Allen and Murray A. Straus, "'Final say' measures of marital power: Theoretical critique and empirical findings from five studies in the United States and India," *Journal of Comparative Family Studies* 15, 3 (1984): 329–344.

43 Robert Rosenthal, *Experimenter Effects in Behavioral Research* (New York: Irvington, 1976): 42–56. For the degree to which this is ignored, see Irwin Silverman, "The experimenter: A (still) neglected stimulus object," *Canadian Psychologist* 15, 3 (1974):258–270.

44 Rosenthal, *Experimenter Effects*, p. 56.

45 See Jessie Bernard, *The Future of Marriage* (New York: Bantam, 1972); Lillian Rubin, *Worlds of Pain: Life in the Working-Class Family* (New York: Basic Books, 1976).

46 Lenore Weitzman, *The Divorce Revolution: The Unexpected Social and Economic Consequences for Women and Children in America* (New York: Free Press, 1985).

47 For example, Thelma McCormack, "Toward a nonsexist perspective on social and political change," in Marcia Millman and Rosabeth Moss Kanter (eds.), *Another Voice* (Garden City, NY: Doubleday, 1975): 1–32; also "Good theory or just theory? Toward a feminist philosophy of social science," *Women's Studies International Quarterly* 4, 1 (1981): 1–12. For empirical evidence see Joni Lovenduski and Jill Hills (eds.), *The Politics of the Second Electorate: Women and Public Participation* (London: Routledge and Kegan Paul, 1981).

48 For example, Jane S. Gaskell, "The reproduction of family life: Perspectives of male and female adolescents," *British Journal of Sociology of Education* 4, 1 (1983): 19–38.

49 Anne B. Shlay and Denise A. DiGregorio, "Same city, different worlds: Examining gender and work based differences in perceptions of neighborhood desirability," Cornell University, unpublished paper, n.d.

50 Charles Sabel and Jonathan Zeitlin, "Historical alternatives to mass production: Politics, markets and technology in nineteenth-century industrialization," *Past and Present* 108 (1985): 133–176.

51 Ibid., pp. 152–153.

52 Ibid., pp. 153–154.

53 Walter Block and Michael A. Walker, *On Employment Equity: A Critique of the Abella Royal Commission Report*. Focus No. 17 (Vancouver: The Fraser Institute, 1985), n. 37, p. 103.

54 Jessie Bernard, *The Future of Marriage* (New York: Bantam Books, 1972):36.

55 Royal Commission on the Economic Union and Development Prospects for Canada, *Report* (Ottawa: Minister of Supply and Services, 1985), 3 vols.

56 This section follows the analysis by Marjorie Cohen, "The MacDonald Report and its implications for women," National Action Committee on the Status of Women, 1985. Reprinted as "Weakest to the wall," *Policy Options* 6, 10 (Dec. 1985).

Chapter 5
Double Standards

5.1 Introduction

A double standard is used when identical behaviors or situations are evaluated, treated, or measured by different criteria. Double standards can be found in language, concepts, methods, interpretation of data, and policy conclusions. The use of a double standard is often difficult to recognize because it is not necessarily introduced along overtly sexual lines, but rather in an indirect manner. Analyzing materials for the existence of a double standard therefore often involves two steps: first, determining whether any sex-based elements are present (whether overtly or indirectly), and second, establishing whether or not the situations discussed are, in fact, comparable.

5.2 Double Standards in Language

5.2.1 Use of Nonparallel Terms for Females and Males

One form of a double standard in language consists of the use of nonparallel terms for males and females in parallel situations. The expression "man and wife" is one example. The phrase should either be "husband and wife" (thus designating both spouses by their marital status) or "man and woman" (thus identifying both by their sex). The custom of referring to females by their first names, while referring to males by their last names is another. For example,

> Olive Schreiner and Havelock Ellis came to know one another during the first half of 1884. Their relationship opened formally, with an admiring but critical letter from Ellis about *African Farm*, and a grateful, rather coy response from Olive. . . . Ellis was born four years after Olive.[1]

One nonsexist way of avoiding this double standard would be to use first and last names for both female and male actors.

5.2.2 *Use of Different Grammatical Modes for the Sexes*

This is a very important problem that goes far beyond the choice of language, but which can be identified easily through language. It is essentially an issue of data interpretation and may be a manifestation of either a double standard (this is certainly the case in straight grammatical terms) or androcentricity. Conceivably, a double standard might also reflect gynocentricity, but again I did not find any examples of this in the literature I reviewed.

To illustrate the problem, let us examine an anthropological description of sex roles and social sanctions in primitive societies:

> Most of the restrictions imposed by primitive societies upon a woman's freedom stem from one or another aspect of her reproductive role. Restrictions connected with pregnancy have been noted, as well as those imposed during the period after childbirth and during lactation. Among many people, limitations are placed upon the activities of women during their menstrual periods as well. Societies vary markedly, however, in the degree to which they curtail a menstruating woman's participation in social life. In a few societies, the only restriction placed upon her activities is that she may not engage in sexual intercourse. In a few other societies, menstruation involves strict seclusion and isolation. The majority of primitive peoples surround the woman with specific restrictions, leaving her free to move about with certain exceptions. Always she is forbidden sexual intercourse, frequently she may not go into the gardens, and may not participate in religious ceremonies.[2]

In this passage, women are consistently described in the passive mode. It is unclear who constitutes "society" (the active agents who place restrictions on women's activities), but according to the text, the women are the passive recipients of these restrictions. It is the grammar of the text that makes us aware that we are dealing with a particular view of the role of women that may or may not be appropriate. This becomes very obvious when we rewrite this passage and identify women as active agents rather than as passive objects to be acted upon. The rewritten passage might read as follows:

Most of the female taboos in primitive societies are directly related to one or another aspect of woman's reproductive role. Pregnancy taboos have been noted as well as post-partum taboos and taboos concerning lactation. Among many peoples, women refrain from certain activities during their menstrual periods as well. Societies vary markedly, however, in the degree to which a woman refuses to participate in social life during menstruation. In a few societies, the only activity she refuses to engage in is sexual intercourse. In a few other societies, menstruation may lead women to completely separate themselves, both physically and socially, from men. In the majority of primitive peoples, women engage only in specific withdrawals and maintain their usual social relations in all other cases. Always, however, the woman refuses to engage in sexual intercourse; frequently, she will not enter the gardens or refuses to cook for men. Her power may be such that, if she touches the man's hunting or fishing gear, calamity may befall him. She will only do so, therefore, if she wishes him ill. Finally, she may refuse to participate in certain religious ceremonies.[3]

The image that emerges from this description is substantially different from the one conveyed in the original passage. Unfortunately, we do not have sufficient information to decide which version is closer to the truth. In such a case, it would be appropriate to write up the information in a neutral manner that does not prejudge who acts and who is acted upon. A version rewritten in this manner might read as follows:

Most of the taboos concerning women in primitive societies are related to one or another aspect of woman's reproductive role. Pregnancy taboos have been noted as well as post-partum taboos and taboos concerning lactation. Among many peoples there are menstrual taboos, as well. Societies vary markedly, however, in the type of menstrual taboos that are prevalent. In a few societies, the only female taboo is one on sexual intercourse. In a few other societies, menstruation involves strict seclusion and isolation. The majority of primitive peoples have specific taboos for women, leaving them free to move about with certain exceptions. Always, there is a sexual intercourse taboo; frequently, there is a gardening taboo, a cooking taboo or a taboo against touching the male's hunting and fishing gear, and a taboo on participation in religious ceremonies.[4]

This version leaves open the question of who acts and who is being acted upon.

It is therefore important to look at the grammatical structure of scholarly writing in order to recognize implicitly sex-related statements that are being made through the language. Writers should write in the active mode about both sexes, rather than treating one sex in the active voice and the other in the passive. Such shifts will certainly require new forms of data collection as well as new interpretations of data already collected. For instance, when dealing with victims, it emphatically does not mean that one may imply – through use of language – that victims cooperate in their victimization. Instead, it means examining the situation from the victim's perspective in order to express the victim's resistance, helplessness, fear, rage, or mute acceptance of the situation. Writing about both sexes in the active voice reinforces the need to examine a given a situation from each sex's perspective.

5.3 Double Standards in Concepts

5.3.1 Concepts Premised on Unequal Treatment of Equal Attributes in the Two Sexes

The most basic form of a double standard in concepts is an unequal treatment of equal attributes for the two sexes. The concept of "head of household" or "family head," often criticized already, provides a good example. This concept continues to be employed by scholars[5] in spite of the various criticisms that have been leveled against it. This concept is often employed without definition (as is the case with the term "family head" in the example cited here), but one assumes it means that only unmarried women living with dependent children and married men are counted as household or family heads, while married women are referred to as "spouses of head" or some such term.

If we reflect for a moment on what we do when we employ such a term, it becomes clear that this is a classic example of a concept based on a double standard. If a woman is married, she becomes the spouse of a head; if a man is married, he becomes the head. If a woman or a man is unmarried, each is a head or "unattached individual" (if no dependents live with them). The same attribute – being married – thus has different consequences for women than it does for men.

This tradition of assigning different labels to men and women stems from a time when men were considered to be the "bread-winners" of their families and wives were considered to be their husbands' dependents. Whether historically the concept was always used appropriately is not a question to be examined here;[6] there is no doubt, however, that it is an inappropriate term for wives who have legal equality with their husbands or independent incomes, whether this be through their earnings or through some other means. On the other hand, for some historical analyses the concept will adequately reflect the social reality of the time.

Identifying all married men as heads of household or family therefore creates not only a double standard for married women; it is also inaccurate when applied to married men who share financial responsibility for their households/families with their wives. A few may even be at home, fulfilling the role traditionally reserved for the "spouse of head." Typically, once such a concept has been introduced and accepted, data analysis is then based on this concept. This means that very different categories may be treated as if they were comparable.

5.3.2 Asymmetrical Concepts

Another form of a double standard at the level of concept formation consists of the coining and use of asymmetrical, one-sided terms. For example, the concept of the "schizophrenogenic mother,"[7] if not coupled with a concept of the "schizophrenogenic father," is asymmetrical, since it directs us to look at the mother for tendencies that may foster schizophrenia and not look at the father. Such asymmetrical concepts can have serious consequences for theory development, as manifested in the pervasive tendency toward mother-blaming in psychological literature. We find two similar instances in the use of, first, the concept of "unwed mother" when it is not coupled with the concept of "unwed father," and second, the term "maternal deprivation" to describe mothers who do not look after their children on a full-time basis, when the equivalent behavior by fathers is not identified as "paternal deprivation."

In order to recognize this type of double standard, we therefore need to ask whether a concept describes a situation, trait, or behavior that could theoretically be found in both sexes. Where the concern is found to be applicable to both sexes but identified with only one, asymmetry exists. The solution is to use a symmetrical pair of concepts (such as schizophrenogenic father and mother, or paternal and maternal deprivation). This implies, of course, that identical research instruments must be used for both sexes.[8]

5.3.3 Value-Laden Concepts

Another form of a double standard in concepts is a differential value judgment of an existing sex difference in a conceptual pair. For example, Dale Spender[9] suggests that the conceptual pair of "field independence" and "field dependence" (that is, ability to be more aware or less aware of a printed number within a particular context) contains a clear value judgment because independence is generally more highly valued than dependence is. This distinction also happens to coincide with a secondary sex difference: men are more likely to be field-independent, while women are more likely to be field-dependent. If we reverse the value judgment, by labeling what is now identified as "field independence" as "context blindness" and changing "field dependence" into "context awareness," the implied value judgment becomes clear.

A similar problem arises with the conceptual pair of "primary earner" and "secondary earner." These terms correspond roughly to employed married men and employed single adults (primary earners) and to employed married women and youths (secondary earners). The value hierarchy is explicitly expressed. In practice this distinction tends to follow sexual lines for married people, although it is sometimes justified by higher income. Since women are unlikely to *choose* to be paid less than men, the categorization thus adds insult to injury. This use of a double standard becomes particularly pernicious when this conceptual pair is utilized to justify the disentitlement of "secondary earners" from certain public programs, such as Unemployment Insurance. At this point we can see how the use of a double standard overlaps with androcentricity, where male interests are maintained at the expense of female interests.

5.4 Double Standards in Methods

5.4.1 Asking Different Questions of the Sexes

In research, we ask questions both in a direct manner and in an indirect manner. If we ask direct questions, we actually address them to a person. More fundamental, however, are the indirect questions underlying such direct questions. These emerge from our research interests and direct our choice of subject matter.

If we find that the sexes are consistently asked different questions even when the circumstances are equivalent, we are dealing with a double standard in the formulation of research questions. For example, children generally have two parents, a mother and a father, but often only the mother's influence on the child's psychosocial development is examined. Such a one-sided approach leads inevitably to one-sided data, which will, inevitably, lead to inappropriate interpretations.

An example of this double standard is found in mother blaming. A recent overview article provides a systematic analysis of psychiatric and psychological journals concerning the etiology of psychopathology by examining how mothers and fathers are treated – differently or the same – in the literature explaining psychopathology.[10] The authors read and classified a total of 125 journal articles; they found that altogether 37,492 (or 72 percent of the total) words were used to describe the mothers, versus 14,416 (28 percent of the total) words used to describe the fathers. Moreover,

> Specific examples of problems in which the mother or the father was mentioned were noted, and a mother:father ratio was computed. That ratio was 346:73 – or almost 5:1 – in the 125 articles. In other words, when authors wanted to illustrate some problem or other, and when they used only mother or father for this purpose, they chose father only 17% of the time.[11]

If we ask different questions of the two sexes, we will receive different answers about them. In 28% of the articles examined, the mother was the only parent investigated for psychopathology or a contribution to the child's problem. This stands in stark contrast to the total absence of articles in which only the father was investigated in this way.

Related to this is that 82% of articles included information about the mother's psychological functioning. Information was given about the father's psychological functioning in 54%. Problems were said to be found with the mother, with no description given of how these conclusions were reached, in 62% of articles; similar reports with respect to the father were found in only 26%.[12]

In addition to the bias introduced by asking different questions about the sexes, implicit questions – those that are not posed directly to respondents by which implicitly underlie the research – can also introduce a double standard. Such a double standard can be difficult to identify because it reveals itself, not in the questions asked, but in the interpretation of the data. For example, a companion article by the same two authors[13] provides examples of the unequal provision of information about mothers and fathers that is due to implicit, unformulated questions. No systematic comparison between the sexes is made; instead, different bits of information are offered for each sex. This is demonstrated in the following quote:

> For instance, at the beginning of a case history, the following was noted: "The father, a brick layer, was 35 yr old when the patient was born. He is healthy. The mother was 33 yr old when the patient was born; she is 'nervous.'" ...[14] The father is described in terms of his occupation, then his age, and then a positive statement about his (apparently physical) health; the mother is described in terms of her age and a negative comment about her emotional functioning. Later in that article, the authors write that the father hit the child and was very dominating and that the patient cried every time he talked about his father and feared that his father did not love him. One can only speculate why, if the father treated his disturbed son this way, the father is described at the start of the case history in terms of his occupation and his physical health, whereas the mother is described only as "nervous." After three case histories – the most vivid by far being the one just described – the authors reached the following conclusion: "Mothers of patients with Klinefelter's syndrome are often overprotective or anxious. ... The behavior disturbance may start at the age of 4–5 if their mothers do not protect them or take care of them.[15]

> Such a conclusion is particularly intriguing in view of the fact that the mothers in the case histories were described as overprotective and anxious, and the only serious psychopathology noted for any parent was that of the father just described.[16]

Thus it is not the questions themselves, but the assumptions implicit in those questions, that introduces the double standard.

5.4.2 *Using Different Research Instruments for the Sexes*

Whenever a study utilizes different instruments for the two sexes, unless it concerns research about a sexually determined biological factor, we are dealing with an application of a double standard. A very obvious example is the use of two different versions of a questionnaire constructed for male and female respondents. This seems to be less common today than it was in the past. However, one way in which a double standard is still routinely practiced in the construction of research instruments hinges on the question of the socioeconomic status of respondents.

The issue of nonsexist approaches to social stratification is a thorny and hotly debated one.[17] At present, no satisfactory alternatives to the current (sexist) approaches have yet been developed, in spite of considerable efforts to that end.[18] Nevertheless, many social scientists continue to use some measure of socioeconomic status or social class that is sexist in some respect. The brief discussion offered here should not be mistaken as an effort to discuss this issue fully.

In the previously discussed article by Dornbush and others on the control of adolescents,

> Each adolescent was assigned to a group in terms of the education of the father or male guardian or, in the absence of a father or male guardian, the education of the mother or female guardian.[19]

In other words, the measurement of education (which is part of the measure of social class used in this article) always carries a value for a male parent or guardian but a zero value for a mother or female guardian when a male counterpart is present. This is particularly problematic when we consider the role of the guardian. Where there is a male guardian, there is no information about whether the child lives with him. Presumably, the child lives with the mother (single fathers were excluded from the study), yet the male guardian is seen as more important in establishing the social class of the adolescent than is the mother with whom the child actually lives.

We learn, further along in the text, that

> when we control for family income, no comparisons are possible within the high-income group because of the limited number of mother-only households with high incomes. ... Repeating this analysis for parental education gives results that are similar to those when family income is the measure of status. Controlling for measures of social class does not affect the consistent relationship between mother-only households and higher rates of adolescent deviance.[20]

It is unclear who or what has been compared with respect to social class: some present fathers versus some absent male guardians versus some present mothers?

As stated, critiques of such practices have been frequent, while solutions to this problem are more difficult to offer. However, in a simple case such as the one offered above, it should be possible to classify both parents in terms of their education, thus avoiding a double standard in measurement through differential treatment of the sexes in the research instrument.

In a specific critique of a similar practice, Judith Hicks Stiehm was able to recompute women's socioeconomic status using an alternative approach.[21] She criticizes Verba and Nie's study of political participation[22] for measuring the socioeconomic status of women and men differently. In the study, women were ranked according to a socioeconomic status index derived from data on (1) education, (2) family income, and (3) occupation of head of household. Stiehm argues:

> The rationale is that SES is not a measure of individual standing but a measure of social access or of offsprings' economic potential. The assumption is that for social activities and economic prediction the family functions as a unit and that the adult male's influence is primary. ... However, most political action is individual action. Only individuals vote or are selected for office. It would seem appropriate, then, that political scientists consider individuals as individuals. After all, a male lawyer, a female lawyer, and the wife of a male lawyer do

not enjoy equal access to political power even if they do enjoy a similar life-style and even if their children do have similar economic opportunities.[23]

She proceeds:

> The conventional way of assigning SES is designed to yield similar male-female status distributions. It is the argument of this paper that if women were assigned SES independent of their male relatives, male and female status distributions would be found to be dissimilar. Specifically, women would almost disappear from the highest SES categories; they would also move out of the lowest categories. Both facts are relevant to thinking about political participation and social policy.[24]

She then reclassifies female respondents in three different ways with respect to their socioeconomic status and finds that in each case the distribution shifts in very important ways, thus substantiating her point.

The problem of inadequate ways to measure socioeconomic status for women and men equally is not really solved by attempts to construct two different measurement instruments.[25] It is helpful to have instruments that are developed from and for female samples only; such instruments – when used in a strictly sex-specific manner – may be useful. If the result is that incumbents of the same occupations are grouped differently depending on their sex, however, we are dealing with another form of a double standard that prevents us from making comparative statements about the relative positions of the sexes.

5.4.3 Coding Procedures

A very blatant example of a double standard in methods consists in coding identical responses differentially by sex. A prominent example of this procedure is provided by the old Strong Vocational Interest Blanks (no longer in use), in which different coding sheets were used to interpret the responses of girls and boys. Boys and girls with identical responses were consequently steered toward different occupations, such as doctor or nurse, on the basis of identical responses. Coding methods should be uniform, as is now the case with these tests.

5.5 Double Standards in Data Interpretation

In section 5.4.1 it was observed that asking different questions of the sexes will inevitably result in distorted data interpretation. Returning to the example used in that section on the scapegoating of mothers in psychological journals, the authors observe of their review of 125 journal articles that

> the father's absence or lack of involvement with the family was noted but not said to contribute to the child's problem in 24% of articles, but in only 2% was the mother's absence or uninvolvement noted but not said to be contributory. ... The child's pathology was attributed at least in part to the mother's activity in 82% of articles, to the mother's inactivity in 43%, to the father's activity in 43%, and to the father's inactivity in 39%.[26]

Other forms of sexism in the design of a study may also lead to a double standard in data interpretation. To return to an example discussed in the chapter on gender insensitivity (the study of Newfoundland migration patterns), we learn that

> male Newfoundlanders residing on the mainland tend to participate more in the work force than do other Canadians or Newfoundlanders remaining at home, while experiencing unemployment rates similar to those of mainlanders. For male returnees to Newfoundland, on the other hand, rates of unemployment are the highest for any provincial group. Moreover, nearly 20 per cent of male returnees eventually drop out of the work force entirely.[27]

While we learn about unemployment among the male emigrants, we do not learn about it among the female emigrants, nor is it clear from the text whether male Newfoundlanders' rates were compared to male mainland rates or to combined male and female mainland rates. This both continues a gender-insensitive analysis and introduces a subtle double standard, insofar as female unemployment is apparently unworthy of attention.

5.6 Double Standards in Policy Evaluations and Recommendations

Policy research in its initial phases can involve all types of sexism. In addition, however, a double standard may enter into the evaluation of existing or proposed policies or recommendations for new policies. It is not always easy to recognize whether a double standard has been applied, since different terms may be used to create the impression that a single standard has been employed. We can thus distinguish between a simple double standard, in which it is obvious that the behavior of the sexes is measured differently, and a complex double standard, in which the same phenomenon occurs but in a less-obvious manner.

5.6.1 Simple Double Standards in Policy Evaluations and Recommendations

Decisions made by judges can be understood as one form of policy interpretation, with the difference that judicial decisions are an application of existing law and have themselves the force of law; the same cannot be said of all policy recommendations. It is all the more important, therefore, to scrutinize judicial decisions for sexism, and in particular, for the existence of a double standard. Several researchers have demonstrated[28] that judges tend to discriminate against mothers involved in custody disputes when they are working for pay. If and when the same activity – in this case, working for pay – is seen in a different light for fathers and for mothers, a simple double standard has been applied.

Another example of a simple double standard in policy recommendations can be found in a recent report on "surrogate" motherhood and other issues submitted by the Ontario Law Reform Commission.[29] Counter to other, similar reports, this report recommends legalizing surrogate motherhood arrangements (in which one woman contracts with a couple to bear a child for them, usually after having been artificially inseminated with the semen of the man, and usually for a fee).

There are many problems with this report, but only one instance of a double standard will be mentioned here. The Commission suggests that the parents involved in such a contractual arrangement be scrutinized by appropriate legal, social, and medical agencies. However, the degrees of scrutiny to be applied to the prospective social parents and to the surrogate mother are so different that they cannot possibly be seen as applying the same standard. For the prospective surrogate mother, recommendation 43 states:

> In assessing the suitability of a prospective surrogate mother, the court should consider, among other factors, her physical and mental health, her marital and domestic circumstances, the opinion of her spouse or partner, if any, and the likely effects of her participation in a surrogate motherhood arrangement upon existing children under her care.[30]

In addition, the parties to the contract "should be required to consider, and to agree upon a resolution" of, among other things, "prenatal restrictions upon the surrogate mother's activities before and after conception, including dietary obligations; and ... conditions under which prenatal screening of the child may be justified or required, for example, by ultrasound, fetoscopy or amniocentesis."[31] This policy represents a massive invasion into the life of the surrogate mother. And the recommendation is unclear about how the prenatal restrictions on the mother would be monitored.

The Commission also recommends that the child be seized from the surrogate mother in case she changes her mind and wishes to keep it. Indeed, the report recommends that "where the court is satisfied that the surrogate mother intends to refuse to surrender the child upon birth, the court, prior to the birth of the child, should be empowered to make an order for transfer of custody upon birth."[32] In a worst-case scenario, such an attitude might lead to virtual imprisonment of the surrogate mother in order to impede her from leaving the country and thus breaking the contractual arrangement.

In comparison to the restrictions on the surrogate mother, the Commission considers a homestudy of the social parents (as is legally required before parents are accepted as prospective adoptive parents) to be too "invasive." Specifically, the report states:

> We believe that the rigorous intervention in the case of adoption by strangers is an inappropriate regulatory model for surrogate mother-hood arrangements. In most cases, we anticipate that such arrange-ments will involve artificial insemination of the surrogate mother by the semen of the male partner of the couple wishing to raise the child. Since he is the natural father of the child, we do not consider it appropriate that he be treated as a stranger, and that he and his partner be subjected to the invasive scrutiny of a homestudy. While there may be occasions where artificial conception technology is employed to achieve a pregnancy where the male is not the natural father, we consider that such cases will be relatively few in number and, therefore, should not affect the view espoused above.[33]

The Commission did eventually recommend that the prospective parents be assessed by the court as to their ability to provide the prospective child with an adequate upbringing,[34] but this "assess-ment" seems in no way comparable to the one that the surrogate mother would have to undergo. When it comes to the rights, obligations, and degree to which scrutiny of her situation seems appropriate to the commission, it seems irrelevant that the surrogate mother is the natural mother of the child in question.[35]

5.6.2 *Complex Double Standards in Policy Evaluations and Recommendations*

For an example of a complex double standard in policy recommen-dations, we shall consider the policy concequences of using a concept based on the conceptual pair of primary and secondary earner (see section 5.3.3). One of the background papers prepared for the MacDonald Commission considered the issue of income security for Canadian workers.[36] In this study, the author proposes some very useful streamlining of the income security system by abandoning a system of personal tax exemptions in favor of a system of universal demogrants. In addition, he also proposes a complete revamping of the Canadian Unemployment Insurance scheme. This restructuring hinges on the classification of unemployed workers as "unemployed employable" (those who would be certified as such and be effectively guaranteed work or, failing that, unemployment insurance); "those who 'cannot' work (the permanently disabled and severely handicapped); and those whom society deems 'should not' or 'need not' work (the elderly and perhaps single parents with preschool children)."[37]

The article is remarkable for its nonsexist language. With the exception of some footnotes (e.g., footnote 66 and 67) in which "wives" and "males" are identified as unemployment insurance recipients, the article speaks about workers, persons, and families. Sex is not presented as a relevant variable in categorizing someone as an unemployed employable or as a person who society deems should not work. It is only through the distinction of secondary and primary earners that a double standard along sexual lines is introduced: "In the majority of cases, secondary workers in families with another full-time worker would not qualify for special employment."[38] They are the "losers," persons who would be displaced from their current unemployment insurance benefits. This "would mainly affect the non-certified unemployed – persons still drawing substantial UI benefits but not awaiting recall, and unemployed persons in families still with one substantial earner."[39] In other words, "Unemployed married workers with a spouse employed full time at average or higher wages will lose net benefits."[40] As a consequence, "Some secondary workers who have been attracted by the current generous UI treatment of unstable and irregular work would withdraw from the labour market, improving job opportunities and perhaps raising wage rates for lower-wage primary workers."[41]

Who are the primary and the secondary workers? While families will be permitted to designate their primary workers, we know that females earn on average 64 percent of what males earn, and thus in the overwhelming majority of cases, the wife will be designated a secondary worker, and the husband a primary worker. The plan in effect amounts to disentitling most wives from drawing unemployment insurance benefits.[42] The double standard – different treatment of married male and female workers – in this case is not simple, since it is not stated in these terms, but rather complex, since it is achieved via a differential conceptual pair, namely that of primary and secondary earner. Recognizing it as a double standard therefore requires recognizing the sexual dimension in the distinction, the double standard inherent in the conceptual pair itself, and the consequences for women and men in the economy.

5.7 Conclusion

As we have seen, recognizing a double standard may not always be easy. In the case of a simple double standard, no major problem exists: when the same responses are coded differently by sex, we are dealing with a very obvious form of the double standard. When dealing with concepts that are attached to one sex only, however, the issue becomes more complicated. In order to decide whether or not a double standard exists, we need to first determine if the quality referred to in the concept also exists in reference to the other sex; by definition, the available literature (provided there is any) will be classified under a different heading. If this is the case, we need to identify a superordinate concept under which two apparently different concepts can be shown to be the same.

In the case of a complex double standard, there are at least two steps involved: (1) identifying some component of the research process (a conceptual pair, a research question, a policy recommendation) as gender-based even though this may not be immediately visible; and (2) identifying whether or not this component is treated by one standard or by a sexual double standard.[43]

Notes

1 Ruth First and Ann Scott, *Olive Schreiner* (New York: Schocken Books, 1980), pp. 124–125.
2 Clellan S. Ford, "Some primitive societies," in Georgene H. Seward and Robert C. Williamson (eds.), *Sex Roles in Changing Society* (New York: Random House, 1970):

25–43, quotation from pp. 22–23. My analysis of this study appeared earlier in Margrit Eichler, *The Double Standard: A Feminist Critique of Feminist Social Science* (London:Croom Helm,1980):22–28.

3 Eichler,*The Double Standard,*pp. 25–26.

4 Ibid., pp. 23–24.

5 For example, Arthur J. Mann, "Economic development, income distribution, and real income levels: Puerto Rico, 1953–1977," *Economic Development and Cultural Change* 33, 3 (1985): 485–502.

6 "The idea of an individual male wage-earner supporting his family was unfamiliar in the first half of the nineteenth century." See Catherine Hakim, "Census reports as documentary evidence: The census commentaries 1801–1951," *Sociological Review* 28, 3 (new series) (1980): 551–580.

7 See A. M. Brodkin, "Family therapy: The making of a mental health movement," *American Journal of Orthopsychiatry* 50, 1 (1980):4–17.

8 There are, of course, some obvious exceptions to this general rule. It would not be a useful question to ask a man how many children he has given birth to. It is, on the other hand, a highly relevant question to ask a man how many biological children he has.

9 Dale Spender, *Man-Made Language* (London: Routledge and Kegan Paul, 1980): 164–165.

10 Paula J. Caplan and Ian Hall-McCorquodale, "Mother-blaming in major clinical journals," *American Journal of Orthopsychiatry* 55, 3 (1985):345–353.

11 Ibid., p. 347.

12 Ibid., p. 349.

13 Paul J. Caplan and Ian Hall-McCorquodale, "The scapegoating of mothers: A call for change," *American Journal of Orthopsychiatry* 55, 4 (1985): 610–613.

14 J. Nielsen, S. Bjarnason, U. Friedrich, A. Froland, V. H. Hansen, and A. Sorensen, "Klinefelter's syndrome in children," *Journal of Child Psychology and Psychiatry* 11 (1970): 109–119, quote from p. 116.

15 Ibid., p. 117.

16 Caplan and Hall-McCorquordale,"Scapegoating," pp. 610–611.

17 For some of the more recent literature on the issue, see Joan Acker, "Women and stratification: A review of recent literature," *Contemporary Sociology* 9 (1980): 23–39; John H. Goldthorpe, "Women and class analysis: In defense of the conventional view," *Sociology* 19, 4 (1983): 475–488; Michelle Stanworth, "Women and class analysis: A reply to Goldthorpe," *Sociology* 18, 2 (1984): 159–170; Anthony Heath and Nicky Britten, "Women's jobs do make a difference: A reply to Goldthorpe," *Sociology* 18, 4 (1984): 475–490; John H. Goldthorpe, "Women and class analysis: A reply to the replies," *Sociology* 18, 4 (1984): 491–499; Robert Erikson, "Social class of men, women and families," *Sociology* 18, 4 (1984): 491–499; Angela Dale, G. Nigel Gilbert, and Sara Arber, "Integrating women into class theory," *Sociology* 19, 3 (1985):384–409.

18 See Acker, "Women," and Monica Boyd and Hugh A. McRoberts, "Women, men, and socioeconomic indendices: An assessment," in Mary G. Powers (ed.), *Measures of Socioeconomic Status: Current Issues.* AAAS Selected Symposium 81 (Boulder, CO: Westview, 1983): 129–159.

19 Sanford M. Dornbush et al., "Single parents, extended households, and the control of adolescents," *Child Development* 56 (1985): 326–341, quotation from p. 328.

Nonsexist Research Methods

Ibid., p. 332.

Judith Hicks Stiehm, "The unit of political analysis: Our Aristotelian hangover," in Sandra Harding and Merrill B. Hintikka (eds.), *Discovering Reality: Feminist Perspectives on Epistemology, Metaphysics, Methodology and Philosophy of Science* (Dordrecht: D. Reidel, 1983): 31–44.

Sidney Verba and Norman Nie, *Participation in America* (New York: Harper & Row, 1972).

Stiehm, "Unit," p. 33.

Ibid., p. 34.

One such example is contained in Dale, Gilbert, and Arber, "Integrating Women," pp. 384–409.

Caplan and Hall-McCorquodale, "Mother-Blaming," p. 349.

Barnett Richling, "'You'd never starve here': Return migration to rural Newfoundland," *Canadian Review of Sociology and Anthropology* 22, 2 (1985): 236–249, quote on p. 238.

See the literature she cites as well as some of the data in Phyllis Chesler, *Mothers on Trial: The Battle for Children and Custody* (New York: McGraw-Hill, 1986).

Ontario Law Reform Commission, *Report on Human Artificial Reproduction and Related Matters* (Toronto: Ministry of the Attorney General, 1985).

Ibid., vol. 2, p. 282.

Ibid., p. 284.

Ibid., p. 252.

Ibid., pp. 234–235.

Ibid., p. 282.

The term "surrogate" mother itself is based on a double standard. It presents the biological mother as a nonmother, while the sperm donor is identified as simply the "father." The heartache that can ensue from such contracts has been vividly played out in the famous case of "Baby M," in which both the contractual mother and the contractual father wanted to have custody of the child. (It was eventually awarded to the father, but the case has been appealed and continues.)

Jonathan R. Kesselman, "Comprehensive income security for Canadian workers," in Francois Vaillancourt (ed.), *Income Distribution and Economic Security in Canada*. Collected Research Studies, Royal Commission on the Economic Union and Development Prospects for Canada (Toronto: University of Toronto Press and Minister of Supply and Services, 1985): 283–319. I would like to thank Monica Townson for drawing my attention to this article. My analysis takes off from hers, in Monica Townson, "Women and the Canadian economy," keynote address to the symposium on Women and the Economy, sponsored by the Canadian Advisory Council on the Status of Women, Ottawa, March 1986.

Ibid., p. 284.

Ibid., p. 295.

Ibid., p. 299.

Ibid., p. 310.

Ibid., p. 311.

The same would be true for unemployed youths, but this is seen as a problem deserving of a special exception: "To relieve severe youth unemployment and reduce incentives for families to fragment, it would be desirable to allow additional family workers such as older dependent children to participate in the employment programs." Ibid., p. 307.

43 There are, of course, double standards that are based on variables other than sex, such as race, age, economic status, and so on. The analysis provided in this chapter should be transferable to such instances, with the appropriate substitutions.

Chapter 6

Sex Appropriateness, Familism, and Sexual Dichotomism

6.1 Introduction

This chapter will deal with the three remaining sexist problems: sex appropriateness, familism, and sexual dichotomism. They have been identified as "derived" not because they are unimportant, but because they can be logically derived from one of the major problems: Sex appropriateness is a subform of a double standard. Familism is an extreme form of gender insensitivity, often in combination with androcentricity. Sexual dichotomism, finally, is an extreme form of a double standard.

They are treated as individual problems here for two reasons: First, these three problems – sex appropriateness, familism, and sexual dichotomism – constitute distinct and well-accepted aspects of contemporary scholarship. It is therefore partially in an attempt to highlight them that they are treated separately rather than as subaspects of the four primary problems. Related to this is the second reason: One of the major aims of this book is to break down sexism in research into manageable components; these components are more easily and clearly identifiable if they have names.

6.2 Sex Appropriateness

Sex appropriateness is a concept based on the assumption that there are behavior patterns or character formations that are more appropriate for one sex than for the other. For example, sex roles are accepted as appropriate (rather than as a manifestation of a double standard). Similarly, it is still widely accepted that sex identity includes a large package of traits that have nothing to do with physical sexual characteristics but everything to do with what is socially constructed as appropriate for the sexes. Indeed, people are seen as deviant or problematic if their conceptions of their proper role or character are broader than what prevailing sex (or gender) roles prescribe. Instead, of course, we should recognize social prescriptions that define certain human traits and behaviors as appropriate for only one sex as the real problem.[1] The assumption of sex appropriateness leads to research approaches and methods that accept existing sex roles as nonproblematic and to the belief that sex-role (gender-role) transcendence is a form of social or psychic disease, rather than a form of mental well-being.

6.2.1 Research Designs Based on Sex Appropriateness

One of the most common ways in which sex appropriateness distorts our understanding of social processes consists in assuming a division of labor in which women are seen as responsible for childcare and home care, while men are simply ignored. For example, a recent article[2] (like many articles before it) examines the impact of maternal employment on children, beginning with the following passage:

> With the increasing number of mothers in the work force, especially among mothers with preschool children, there is a need to understand how this important social change affects children. The present investigation examines one way in which the maternal employment situation may influence the socialization process. More explicitly, why mothers are working outside the home and what employment means to mothers are addressed as possible powerful influences on how mothers think about their children.[3]

I have yet to read a study that begins with the following statement:

> With the high number of fathers in the work force especially among fathers with preschool children, there is a need to understand how this important social phenomenon affects children. The present investigation examines one way in which the paternal employment situation may influence the socialization process. More explicitly, why fathers are working outside the home and what employment means to fathers are addressed as possible powerful influences on how fathers think about their children."[4]

This study could have been very interesting if the author had asked both parents about their work experiences and how these affect their relationship with their children. Instead, we learn that both parents were asked, in interviews,[5] about sources of satisfaction and stress:

> Two of the sources of satisfaction and stress assessed were parents' feelings about their children and, for those mothers working outside the home, their employment. ... Some examples of items dealing with maternal employment are: "How do you feel about working?" "How does this work out so far as you and your child are concerned?" and "Are there things about your job that you particularly like or dislike?"[6]

Apparently fathers and housewives/mothers were asked different questions. We are confronted here with an assumption of sex appropriateness: childcare is seen as a maternal role, and not as a paternal role. This leads to a double standard in methods, in which different questions are asked of the sexes although the situations are comparable (both mothers and fathers had paid jobs). The effect of this approach is that the relationship between employed mothers and children is made problematic, while the relationship between employed fathers and their children, as well as that between housewife-mothers and their children, is implicitly seen as nonproblematic. Ultimately, this leads to a form of mother-blaming in the data interpretation: Mothers employed full-time

> couched their sons' activity in negative terms. Further, they described their sons as being demanding and noncompliant. Such terms seem congruent with the notion that full-time maternal employment may compound the undersocialization of sons. ... This interpretation lends partial support to the hypotheses put forth by Hoffman ... that greater undersocialization may account for the poorer academic performance of sons whose middle-class mothers are employed.[7]

Where in all of this is the father? It appears that he has no implicit duty to socialize his son. The mother is once again guilty.

In this particular study, the interviews were open-ended, so the exact wording of questions (except in the style as cited above) is not available. The same problem may, of course, appear in studies that use a structured interview approach, as in the following example. In this study,[8] which examined the daily lives of women in 538 Toronto families, we find a set of questions that are also premised on some notion of sex appropriateness:

- What do you think is different in your children's day because you have a job? (asked of the mother)

- If your children have to get in touch with you at work, how easy or difficult is it for them to reach you?

- How often do you feel a conflict between being a mother and "working"?[9]

The implication is that a conflict exists as a result of the mother's paid work but not of the father's paid work. These questions could have been asked of both sexes; of course, this would have meant interviewing both sexes, thus doubling the sample, complicating the study, and probably increasing costs. But the result would have been a more informative and reliable study about family/work conflict.[10] It is important also to note here that granting agencies might question the increased costs of broadening the study. It is therefore essential not only for academic researchers themselves to become aware of sexism in research, but also to educate granting agencies on this score in order to encourage funding for nonsexist research.

Another recent article[11] tries to explain wives' labor force participation by examining the relative impact of attitudinal factors and family economic resources. The analysis is based on data from the Edmonton Area Study, consisting of responses to four questions that are identified as "gender-related issues."[12] The four questions are as follows:

(1) Do you approve or disapprove of "a married woman working, if she has pre-school age children and a husband capable of supporting her."

(2) Do you agree or disagree that "housework is more rewarding than having an outside job."

(3) that "a woman is likely to feel unfulfilled unless she becomes a mother."

(4) that "a husband should be entirely responsible for earning the living for a family (under normal circumstances)."[13]

Three of these four questions (1, 3, and 4) are premised on a notion of sex appropriateness. Question 2 is nonsexist, since it is couched in general terms. The other questions all assume a division of labor in which it is considered problematic if the mother has paid employment or the father is not the sole economic provider. These questions could be made nonsexist by coupling them with equivalent questions about the other person. In particular, Question 3 (about the importance of motherhood for a woman) must be coupled with a question about the importance of fatherhood for a man in order to yield meaningful information. *Only* when we know about the reactions of both sexes to being a parent can we draw any inferences whatsoever about parenthood as a gender-related issue. It is quite conceivable that both a male and a female respondent may hold strong notions about parenthood that have nothing whatsoever to do with any assumed sex appropriateness. However, by asking only one-sided questions, such an interpretation is not possible because half the necessary data are missing.

Another recent study[14] demonstrates how asking questions about sex-appropriate behavior in a nonsexist manner can produce quite different results. In this case, blue-collar women and men, white-collar women and men, male and female teachers, and male and female decision makers were asked to agree or disagree with the following statement:

If a married woman has to stay away from home for long periods of time in order to have a career, she had better give up the carer.[15]

Fifty-nine percent of the male and 65 percent of the female blue-collar workers agreed with the statement, as opposed to 34 percent of the male and 13 percent of the female decision makers.[16] It would be reasonable to interpret such a finding to mean that female blue-collar workers have the most conservative notions about their sex roles, with the majority of them perceiving a conflict between career and family for a married woman with children.

These respondents were also asked to agree or disagree with the following statement:

If a married man has to stay away from home for long periods of time in order to have a career, he had better give up the career.[17]

This time we find that 34 percent of the male and 49 percent of the female blue-collar workers agreed with this statement, as opposed to 25 percent of the male and 13 percent of the female decision makers.

Subsequently, a so-called double standard score was computed to assess how many people would want a married woman to give up her career without wanting a married man to give up his career, and vice versa. This was achieved by cross-tabulating the responses to both questions. The results are fascinating: 25 percent of male and 12 percent of female blue-collar workers, and 9 percent of male and 0 percent of female decision makers exhibited a double standard with respect to their family and career expectations for women and men.

By asking both sides of the question rather than assuming sex appropriateness, we thus arrive at a totally different conclusion. Now the male blue-collar workers appear to be the most conservative group, albeit to a significantly lesser degree than our first interpretation suggested. The female blue-collar workers appear to have responded to the first question in the way they did, not because of adherence to traditional sex roles, but because they place a higher value on family life than on work life for *both* spouses.

6.2.2 *Policy Recommendations Premised on Notions of Sex Appropriateness*

In an otherwise interesting article[18] on fathers' birth attendance and their involvement with their newborns, the author in effect ends up arguing that traditional sex roles that do not involve the father in direct parenting should be recognized professionally as an acceptable option. He suggests:

> Researchers need to realize that paternal support can be represented by a wide range of behaviours, and that families most likely adopt patterns of interaction maximizing the match between roles, skills, and needs. The implication is that in some cases the optimal pattern of paternal support may involve little direct participation in child care. Perhaps investigators would do well to examine broad patterns of paternal involvement (e.g. support of the mother) rather than focussing on specific aspects of fathering behaviour (e.g. number of diapers changed).[19]

This thought is strongly reinforced in the conclusion:

> What is required is a balanced approach where fathers, in consultation with their partners, choose at all stages of the parenting process levels of involvement that are consistent with their skills, desires, and perceived roles.

> A father's attitudes concerning his sex role, the fathering role, the support he receives from his partner, and other related variables exert considerable impact on paternal involvement. ... Among the most productive goals that we as professionals can have is to facilitate a realistic, positive perception of a wide range of paternal roles in relation to pregnancy, birth, and the transition to parenthood.[20]

Initially children have an absolute need for care that exists independent of their parents' skills, desires, and perceived roles. Since the author makes no statements about the mother's skills, desires, and perceived roles, he presumably wishes to offer choice to fathers, thus potentially reducing choice to mothers – assuming that if fathers choose not to participate in the caring process, mothers will be left with doing it on their own.

6.2.3 Sex-Role Transcendence as a Form
of Mental Illness

Returning one more time to the previously cited review of 125 journal articles on the etiology of psychopathology,[21] we learn that

> moving to reviews of the literature in the articles studied, in 28% a traditional division of labour was explicitly regarded as normal and

healthy, and deviation from it was assumed to be pathogenic. Nontraditional division of labour was never regarded as normal and healthy. Traditional sex roles (in terms of behavior) and traditional family structures (two-parent, heterosexual) were regarded as normal and healthy, and any deviation from this as pathogenic in 43% of articles. In no article was the converse true.[22]

In other words, in nearly half of the literature surveyed, the authors found that sex-role transcendence was considered to be deviant.

6.2.4 Sex Appropriateness as a Sexist Problem

It would be interesting to examine how many recent introductory textbooks in sociology and psychology still discuss sex or gender roles and sex or gender identity in terms of "appropriate" behavior and socialization. To the degree that the term "sex appropriate" is seen as an acceptable yardstick against which to measure and judge behavior, we are dealing with a form of sexism. This does not mean that the concepts of sex role or sex identity should be eliminated. They remain useful *descriptive* (but not prescriptive or explanatory) terms. Sex appropriateness appears not only when the labels are present, but also when research designs or data interpretation are guided by the notion that there are sets of behaviors or traits that are appropriate for one sex but not for the other.[23] Instead, behaviors and traits should be judged by criteria other than which sex engages in or displays them.

6.3 Familism

6.3.1 Introduction

Familism is a specific form of gender insensitivity. It consists of taking the family as the smallest unit of analysis in cases in which it is in fact *individuals*, or a collection of individuals, who engage in particular actions.[24] The use of families or households as the smallest unit of analysis is, of course, not always sexist. There is nothing problematic about providing particular definitions of a household or family and assessing, for example, how many households or families in a country fall into these categories, or how many households are affected by particular tax provisions, and so on. A problem does exist, however, when an action or experience is attributed to a family or household when in fact the action is carried out, or the event is potentially differentially experienced, by individuals within the unit; or when the family is credited with properties that are actually the aggregate properties of the individuals within it. A problem also exists when households or families are treated as a unit, the members of which suffer or profit equally from events that in fact have a differential impact on different members.

6.3.2 *Attribution of Individual Actions, Experiences, or Properties to the Household/Family*

We find quite frequently that households are assumed to do things that are in fact performed by individuals within them (and by no means all individuals within them). Economic analyses in particular tend to assume that households make decisions, buy and sell, react or fail to react to constraints and opportunities, and so on.

For example, we read that "households make joint decisions about their portfolios of assets and their labour supply, choosing among the labour contracts offered by the different firms."[25] Or we read about the "buying effort by households."[26] And "the household that buys Y and sells N gets to consume. ... thus the household's decision problem ... the household's profit income ... all of which the household takes as given."[27] This approach hides the fact that women and men tend to participate differentially in decisions that affect the household and the family,[28] and that what is presented as something decided by the household or family may, in fact, have been decided against the wishes of, and/or to the detriment of, one or more of its members.

Nor do households or families per se engage in actions. For instance, when scholars write that "families" care for their children and for the aged, in effect they attribute individual actions to the unit as a whole. For example,[29]

When gerontologists do discuss the more concrete tasks and

activities which constitute family involvement with the elderly, they invoke a language which obscures the feminine nature of that care. Nowhere has this been more evident than in studies of the frail and ill elders, where euphemisms abound for care provided by women in families. Brody[30] claims the phrase "alternatives to institutions" should be read "daughter" of the elderly person. Chappell[31] amends that to "daughter or wife." Framed in public language, or that of large scale organizations rather than domestic groups, the private actions of individual women engaged in caring for older members of their family are translated into "family support systems"[32] and "family as a health service organization."[33]

This is not the only way in which familism may manifest itself. In psychology and sociology, we sometimes find the assumption that parents always act as a unit and in concert when in fact this may not be the case. For instance, in one particular study children were asked:

> Do you have any ideas about the sort of job you'd like to do when you leave school? What do you think your parents would like you to do when you leave school?[34]

This question presupposes that both parents have an idea of what they want their child to do after he or she has finished school, and that they agree on this issue. What happens if Dad wants his child to become a nurse while Mom wants her to become a statistician? The simple solution to this problem is, of course, to ask two questions in order to identify whether or not the parents' wishes are identical (what would your mother like you to become? . . . your father?) and to proceed in the analysis from there.

A parallel problem consists in attributing an individual property to the entire unit in cases in which members of the unit do not necessarily equally own or display this property. A simple example of this type of familism occurs when racial or ethnic family membership is determined on the basis of only one of the family members' background, such as when a family in which the husband/father is Pakistani, while the wife/mother is Dutch, is classified as Pakistani rather than as mixed Pakistani/Dutch. If the family were classified as Dutch it would, of course, be exactly the same problem.[35]

This type of sexism also occurs when the incomes of the individual family members are treated as "family income." This would be appropriate if all family members were legally and socially entitled equally to the income of all family members. Since this is generally not the case, however, it is inappropriate unless the data are presented in disaggregated as well as aggregated form. This issue leads us to the next manifestation of familism.

6.3.3 Attribution of Equal Benefit or Detriment to the Members of a Family Unit

We know from several studies that husbands and wives do not, in fact, have equal say over money earned by one of the spouses.[36] In policy studies in particular, it is very important to keep in mind who within a family unit generates income, and who has control over it. We cannot assume that a particular amount of money is necessarily of equal benefit to all members, irrespective of who controls it. To return to the example on unemployment insurance used in Chapter 5, the Commission proposed that "secondary earners" be disentitled from unemployment benefits on the basis of "family income." (The primary earner's income refers in most cases to the husband's income.) By treating the husband's income as family income, this policy would in effect disentitle the secondary earner (i.e., the wife) from her personally earned benefits on the assumption that she shares this income of her husband. Loss of job would thus be compounded by loss of earned unemployment insurance benefits.

The assumption of equal benefits is often expressed by such terms as "joint utility functions" or "optimization." For instance,

> Barro has argued that it may be optimal for households to react to an increased deficit by increasing their saving by an equal amount. Consequently, neither aggregate demand nor interest rates may rise. Households will so react if capital markets are perfect, if they understand the intertemporal budget constraints they face, and if they have operative altruistic intergenerational transfer motives.[37]

What is sexist about this approach? The bold assertion that something is "optimal" for a household when it may in fact have quite different effects on the various household members. One analysis that empirically tested the assumption of joint utility maximizing is Folbre's study of Philippine households.[38]

> Folbre rejects Becker's assertion of an altruistic, but nevertheless joint-utility maximizing unit where individual preferences are consistent with maximizing family welfare. Analysis of the data on family expenditures on various members revealed that women received less than the accepted levels of nutrition and men received more. Girls had much less time spent on them than boys, and after the age of nine more of the family income was allocated to sons.[39]

6.3.4 Familism as a Sexist Problem

Many researchers routinely talk about the family as if the unit as a whole experienced or did things in the same manner, or as if any differences in the impact on, or activities of, individual family members are irrelevant. This is a particularly entrenched form of gender insensitivity that has a pervasive impact on policy formation in particular. A judgment that a particular policy (action, experience, benefit) is good for the entire family unit must in all cases be preceded by a study that examines the effects of such policy on *each* member. Only when it has been demonstrated (not assumed) that the effect is beneficial – or at least not detrimental – to each and every family member can the statement be made that it is "good for the family."

Familism may also distort the attribution of properties to families. In cases in which the experiences (traits, behaviors) of male and female family members are disparate, ignoring such differences will create a picture that is inaccurate for one or both. It is like a couple that wishes to buy one suit that they can both wear. If one of them is four feet tall, and the other six feet tall, their joint height would be five feet. If they, accordingly, buy a "family suit" for a five-foot-tall person, it will fit neither one. Collective attribution of *any* property should therefore be made only after the individuals' attributes have been examined and found to coincide.

6.4 Sexual Dichotomism

6.4.1 Introduction

Sexual dichotomism is an extreme form of a double standard. It consists of treating the sexes as two discrete, rather than overlapping, groups.[40] It is neither a new problem, nor a newly recognized one, but it has become more common. It tends to appear when researchers attempt to avoid another form of sexism: gender insensitivity. Sexual dichotomism is certainly not gender insensitive; on the contrary, sexual dichotomism occurs when gender sensitivity is perverted into a form of scholarly gender apartheid.

Sexual dichotomism may manifest itself in concepts as well as in the overall research design. In general, whenever we postulate categorical social distinctions between the sexes, we are engaging in sexual dichotomism.[41]

6.4.2 Sexual Dichotomism in Concepts

In cases in which human attributes are identified with one sex or the other, a form of sexual dichotomism results. The identification of estrogen and testosterone as "female" and "male" hormones, respectively, is a case in point. Both females and males have estrogen and testosterone in their bodies, albeit in quite different proportions.

This issue becomes more important when dealing with character attributes. There are "generally recognized" character attributes that are seen as masculine or feminine, such as independence or leadership capacity (on the masculine side), or emotionality or sensitivity (on the feminine side). Since both males and females can (and do) display these attributes, albeit in different proportions, the characterization of these traits as masculine or feminine suggests that their display in the other sex is somehow "unnatural."

6.4.3 Sexual Dichotomism in the Research Design

A preeminent example of sexual dichotomism occurs when part or all of a research design is premised on the notion that the sexes are discrete groups. Masculinity–femininity scales are one such example. The most famous of these scales is part of the Minnesota Multiphasic Personality Inventory (MMPI). The "MMPI is the most used psychological test in the world. Its results are analyzed and interpreted thousands of times daily."[42]

> Profiles generated by testee responses to the instrument's items are often given great credibility in diagnosing pathology and categorizing personality traits. It can be assumed that decisions affecting people's lives are often made based, at least in part, on the interpretation of these profiles.[43]

One part of the instrument, the so-called scale five, is a masculinity–femininity scale. Its original objective was to identify "homosexual invert males."[44] Attempts to make the scale serve this purpose, and to use it to distinguish female homosexuals from "normals," were not successful.

The scale was also designed to discriminate between men and women. A recent evaluation of the utility of the scale states categorically:

> Clearly the MMPI Mf scale does not do what it was intended to do. It does not measure homosexuality in any clearcut way nor does it measure characteristics that reliably divide males from females.[45]

Nevertheless, "scores on Scale Five have come to be routinely reported in the MMPI profile."[46]

In fact, researchers are still constructing new scales from the items contained in the MMPI. One recent effort involves the construction of a scale purportedly measuring a "gender dysphoria syndrome" in males, the "Gd" scale.[47] The Gd scale consists of 31 items that represent three factors: identification with stereotypic feminine interests; denial of male interests; and affirmation of excellent physical and mental health.[48]

Leaving aside for a moment the paradox that affirmation of excellent physical and mental health is taken as one indicator of what is perceived as a gender identity disorder, responses that are seen as indicative of this disorder include affirmation of the following items:

- I enjoy reading love stories.
- I would like to be a nurse.
- I like collecting flowers or growing house plants.
- I like to cook.
- If I were a reporter I would very much like to report news of the theater.
- I used to like hopscotch.
- I think I would like the work of a dressmaker.
- I would like to be a private secretary.

Among the responses that indicate the presence of the disorder are negation of the following items:

- I like mechanics magazines.
- I think I would like the work of a building contractor.
- If I were a reporter I would very much like to report sporting news.
- I like or have liked fishing very much.
- I like adventure stories better than romantic stories.

Using these items, males will be judged to suffer from a personality disorder when they admit to liking to cook, being interested in theatre news, liking flowers and houseplants, and so on, while failing to like mechanics magazines, fishing, and being interested in sports news. They must also profess excellent physical and mental health to be judged as having a psychological disorder. "Any individual with a raw score of 17 or above on the Gd scale would be viewed as having a high probability of a diagnosis of gender dysphoria."[49]

This scale represents an extreme form of sexual dichotomism. Certain characteristics (human attributes) found in both males and females are classified as either masculine or feminine on the basis of prevailing stereotypes in a given society at a certain point in time.[50] The fact that some males display these attributes is not taken as an indication of inappropriate labeling. The sexual dichotomy that has been artificially created is accorded more weight than reality itself is. Indeed, the authors suggest that "the greatest usefulness of the scale may lie in its potential for identifying and predicting gender identity conflicts in a *nonascribed* gender dysphoric patient population. ... Once these patients' gender identity conflicts are identified, they can be appropriately assigned for treatment."[51] In other words, those poor men who did not know that they were sick, believing themselves in excellent mental and physical health, and having a range of interests and skills that is greater than that of many other men, could finally be cured of this affliction. Including the concept of androgyny in the construction of Mf scales does not solve the problem of sexual dichotomism, as has been shown elsewhere.[52]

In anthropology, we not infrequently find analytical frameworks that dichotomize the sexes and associate the dichotomy with other – also dichotomized – concepts. Such a scheme might look as follows:[53]

male	:	female
culture	:	nature
public	:	domestic
production	:	reproduction
agent	:	object
articulate	:	inarticulate
superior	:	inferior
active	:	passive
authority	:	influence

The problem is compounded when such frameworks are given the status of universal applicability and significance.[54]

6.4.4 Sexual Dichotomism in Methods

Gd scales are not the only way in which sexual dichotomism may manifest itself. Certain methods may also result in sexual dichotomism. To provide just one example: The manner in which tests of significance are sometimes used may result in sexual dichotomism. This is not to say that the use of tests of significance is sexist, but merely that they may be used in a sexist manner.

In a conventional test of significance, there are three basic steps:

> (1) The researcher sets up a null hypothesis ... which he or she is typically interested in rejecting in favour of the research hypothesis. ... (2) A probability model is specified. ... (3) The test statistic is computed, and a decision made about whether or not to reject the null hypothesis.[55]

Since theories cannot, in principle, be proven, researchers utilizing such techniques will concentrate on rejecting false alternatives. "While the null hypothesis does not necessarily have to assume 'no difference' ... the practise is so common that textbooks often define the null hypothesis in this way."[56] Tests of significance group all effects into two classes: present or absent. As applied to gender differences, the inference drawn is that the specific gender difference under investigation either exists or does not exist. Given that the null hypothesis is usually "no difference," rejecting the null hypothesis results in an affirmation of the existence of a difference. In a cumulative sense, this may have a very peculiar effect.

> Findings are defined as significant at some specified level if the null hypothesis is rejected. The inference is drawn that some 'cause' is at work. Alternatively, if it appears that chance alone might have produced the sample results, no other explanation is thought necessary. A non-significant finding is rarely regarded as a refutation of the research hypothesis; instead the usual conclusion is that the study failed to establish that the differences were there. The success of the research as measured in terms of significance tests influences the chances that the report will be published. Therefore, in a cumulative manner, sex differences are exaggerated. Tresemer[57] argues that there is a "great iceberg" of studies, unpublished because

of their inability to reject the hypothesis of no difference, that never come to light or that do not report their results separately by sex.

Finally, significance tests are often misinterpreted as measures of importance or substantive significance.[58]

In this instance, therefore, a particular statistical technique, if applied to gender differences in the described manner, is likely to exaggerate sex differences over similarities. In other words, it will exaggerate the importance of gender as a categorical variable. Wherever techniques have this effect, we are dealing with a case of sexual dichotomism in methods.[59]

6.4.5 Sexual Dichotomism as a Form of Sexism

Just as a complete de-sexing of language may be misperceived as being nonsexist, so sexual dichotomism may be mistaken as a remedy for gender insensitivity. Avoiding one mistake by making another does not make things any better, however. Whenever the sexes are treated as categorically different groups in instances in which *human* attributes are assigned to one or the other sex, sexual dichotomism results.

6.5 Conclusion

Sex appropriateness, familism, and sexual dichotomism are three common problems in research. Sex appropriateness consists of taking a set of historical assumptions about the "proper" behavior and the nature of the sexes and giving them a normative status. Familism consists of attributing individual properties to the family unit or ignoring relevant intrafamilial differentiation. Sexual dichotomism, finally, consists of treating the sexes as two discrete groups, rather than as overlapping groups, by attributing human properties to only one sex and by ignoring intragroup differences. It is thus a modern version of biologism, which treats a biological variable (sex) as if it were a social variable.

The solution to this latter problem is emphatically not, as has been proposed, to stop "seeing two genders."[60] We must be gender sensitive *and* avoid falling into the trap of sexual dichotomism, or, to turn it around, we must avoid sexual dichotomism *and* avoid falling into the trap of gender insensitivity. If we fail, we will only have substituted one sexist problem for another.

Notes

1 For an extensive discussion of the inherent sexism in the use of sex (gender) roles or sex (gender) identity as *explanatory* rather than descriptive variables, see Margrit Eichler, *The Double Standard: A Feminist Critique of Feminist Social Science* (London: Croom Helm, 1980), chaps. 2 and 3.

2 William F. Alvarez, "The meaning of maternal employment for mothers and their perceptions of their three-year-old children," *Child Development* 56, 2 (1985): 350–360.

3 Ibid., p. 350.

4 There is an emergent literature on fathers and an incipient realization that the employment situation of fathers does very much affect the socialization process; however, this particular article does not display such knowledge, nor do many others.

5 Ibid., p. 352.

6 Ibid.

7 Ibid., p. 356.

8 William Michelson, *From Sun to Sun: Daily Obligations and Community Structure in the Lives of Employed Women and Their Families* (Totowa, NJ: Rowman and Allanheld, 1985).

9 Ibid., p. 199.

10 I am using this particular study as an example because it is (a) important, (b) recent, and (c) has the advantage of presenting the complete survey instrument within the book, a practice that is unfortunately not always followed, making the type of criticism engaged in here impossible. Ironically, some of the better studies thus get singled out for criticism rather than more grossly biased ones.

11 Graham S. Lowe and Harvey Krahn, "Where wives work: The relative effects of situational and attitudinal data," *Canadian Journal of Sociology* 10, 1 (1985): 1–22.

12 Ibid., p. 10.

13 Ibid., p. 11, t. 1.

14 Margrit Eichler, *Families in Canada Today: Recent Changes and their Policy Consequences* (Toronto: Gage, 1983).

15 Ibid., p. 67.

16 Ibid., p. 68.

17 Ibid., p. 71.

18 Rob Palkovitz, "Fathers' birth attendance, early contact, and extended contact with their newborns: A critical review," *Child Development* 56, 2 (1985): 392–406.

19 Ibid., p. 398.

20 Ibid., p. 405.

21 Paula J. Caplan and Ian Hall-McCorquodale, "Mother-blaming in major clinical journals," *American Journal of Orthopsychiatry* 55, 3 (1985): 345–353.

22 Ibid., pp. 349–350.

23 There are, of course, many behaviors and traits that are not appropriate for anybody, such as unprovoked violence.

24 I am here treating the use of families or households as units of analysis as indicative of the same problem, rather than as distinct issues. One might call the problem "householdism" when the term household is used, but this would add nothing but another ugly neologism.

25 Jacques H. Dreze, "(Uncertainty and) the firm in general equilibrium theory," *Supplement to the Economic Journal* 95 (1985):14.

26 Peter Howitt, "Transaction costs in the theory of unemployment," *American Economic Review* 7, 5 (March 1985): 192.

27 Ibid., p. 94.

28 See the vast literature on family decision-making. A few references (from which many other references can be gleaned) include Robert J. Meyer and Robert A. Lewis, "New wine from old wineskins: Marital power research," *Comparative Family Studies* 7, 3 (1976): 397–407; Wayne Hill and John Scanzoni, "An approach for assessing marital decision-making processes," *Journal of Marriage and the Family* 44, 4 (1982): 927–941; Craig M. Allen, "On the validity of relative validity of 'final-say' measures of marital power," *Journal of Marriage and the Family* 46, 3 (1984): 619–629.

29 The following quote is from Emily M. Nett, "Family studies of elders: Gerontological and feminist approaches." Paper presented at the annual meeting of the Canadian Sociology and Anthropology Association, 1982, pp. 10–11.

30 E. Brody, "Innovative programs and services for elderly and the family." Testimony before the Select Committee on Aging, U.S. House of Representatives, 96th Congress, Washington, D.C., 1980.

31 Neena L. Chappell, "The future impact of the changing status of women." Plenary address presented at the research workshop on Canada's Changing Age Structure: Implications for the Future, Burnaby, B.C., 1981.

32 J. Treas, "Family support systems for the aged: Some social and demographic considerations," *Gerontologist* 17 (1977): 486–491.

33 Victor W. Marshall, Carolyn J. Rosenthall, and Jane Synge, "The family as a health service organization for the elderly." Paper presented at the annual meeting of the Society for the Study of Social Problems, Toronto, 1981.

34 Judith A. Cashmore and Jacqueline J. Goodnow, "Agreement between generations: A two-process approach," *Child Development* 56, 2 (1985): 495.

35 Until 1981, the Canadian census reported only the respondent's paternal ancestry. This was changed, starting with the 1981 census. See Canada, *1981 Census Dictionary* (Ottawa: Minister of Supply and Services, 1982): 15.

36 See Meredith Edwards, *Financial Arrangements within Families: A Research Report for the National Women's Advisory Council* (Canberra: 1981). Edwards provides other references to the literature.

37 Paul Evans Alson, "Do large deficits produce high interest rates?" *American Economic Review* 75, 1 (March 1985): 85.

38 N. Folbre, "Household production in the Phillipines: A non-neoclassical approach," *Economic Development and Cultural Change*, Working Paper 26 (1983): 1–31. The discussion in this section follows Margaret A. White, "Breaking the circular hold: Taking on the patriarchal and ideological biases in traditional economic theory." OPSPA Paper 7, Women's Studies Centre, OISE, Toronto, 1984.

39 White, "Breaking the Circular Hold," p. 12.

40 Ruth Hershberger, *Adam's Rib* (New York: Harper & Row, 1970), makes this point in a most amusing manner. See particularly n. 1 on pp. 203–212 on the concept of "normality."

41 We are also falling into a primitive form of biologism, a point made by R. W. Connell in "Theorizing gender," *Sociology* 19, 2 (1985): 260–272. He points toward a curious paradox that ensues when assuming the stance of sexual dichotomism (he does not use this term):

> a social fact or process is coupled with, and implicitly attributed to, a biological fact. The result is not only to collapse together a rather heterogeneous group (do gays suffer from malestream thought, for instance; or boys?). It also, curiously, takes the heat off the open opponents of feminism. The hard-line male chauvinist is now less liable to be thought personally responsible for what he says or does in particular circumstances, since what he says or does is attributable to the general fatality of being male. (p. 266)

42 Martin R. Wong, "MMPI Scale Five: Its meaning, or lack thereof," *Journal of Personality Assessment* 48, 3 (1984): 279–284, quote on p. 282.

43 Ibid., p. 279.

44 Ibid.

45 Ibid., p. 280.

46 Ibid.

47 Stanley A. Althof, Leslie M. Lthstein, Paul Jones, and John Shen, "An MMPI Subscale (Gd): To identify males with gender identity conflicts," *Journal of Personality Assessment* 47, 1 (1983): 42–49.

48 Ibid., p. 47.

49 Ibid., p. 48.

50 It strikes one as particularly ironic that skills like cooking are included in the scale, given the current high degree of divorce in North America and the likely attendant need for men to cook for themselves. In my opinion, cooking should be seen as a necessary survival skill for every human adolescent and adult. I would class its lack as a social and psychological problem for any adult, male or female.

51 Ibid., p. 48.
52 See Margrit Eichler, *The Double Standard* (London: Croom Helm, 1980): 69–71.
53 Joanne C.J. Prindiville, "When is a mother not a mom? Reflections on the contributions of cross-cultural studies to models of sex and gender." Unpublished paper, delivered at the CRIAW Conference, Vancouver, 1983, p. 6.
54 Ibid.
55 Rhonda Lenton, "What statisticians can learn from feminists and feminists from statisticians." Unpublished paper, Dept. of Sociology, McMaster University, 1986.
56 Ibid.
57 David Tresemer, "Assumptions made about gender roles," in Marcia Millman and Rosabeth Moss Kanter (eds.), *Another Voice* (Garden City, NY: Anchor Books, 1975): 308–339.
58 Lenton, "What statisticians can learn."
59 There are, of course, other instances of such usage. For example, box score tallies can be used such that they distort sex differences as well as similarities; see Paula J. Caplan, "Beyond the box score: A boundary condition for sex differences in aggression and achievement striving," *Progress in Experimental Personality Research* 9 (1979):41–87.
60 Sarah H. Matthews, "Rethinking sociology through a feminist perspective," *The American Sociologist* 17, 1 (1982): 29–35.

Chapter 7
Guidelines for
Nonsexist Research

7.1 Introduction

So far, we have identified four major and three derived sexist
problems. We have looked at concrete examples as they appear in
the literature, sometimes in rather gross form, sometimes in more
subtle form. The point of identifying sexism in research is, of course,
to eliminate it. This chapter will, to that end, provide a framework
for conducting nonsexist research. The guidelines proposed here
can be applied to an individual piece of research – either one's own
or someone else's. They are relevant both when formulating a
research project and when evaluating a finished piece of research.
And they are applicable to all of the social sciences.

The various types of sexist problems have been sufficiently
discussed in the preceding chapters. It is worth reiterating one

important point, however: This book is intended not to help you "correctly" identify a type of sexism in a given piece of work but to identify sexism *in some way* and to overcome it without falling into a different mode of sexist thinking.

This chapter and the checklist included in the Appendix are organized by component of the research process. Just as the various sexist problems tend to occur together, so too the various components of the research process overlap. It is nevertheless helpful to break the research process down into components in order to group various questions together.

It is also difficult to identify the various stages of the research process in a manner that is applicable to a wide range of approaches. Although there is some logical progression to the way in which this chapter is organized – I begin with the title (which is usually the first thing one reads) and conclude with policy evaluations and recommendations (which, if they exist, are usually the last part of a study) – we should not think of these stages as exclusively sequential. For example, in order to assess whether or not a title is overgeneral, we must be familiar with the entire content of a study. Similarly, concepts are such a fundamental aspect of research that they are invariably used in the earliest stages of the research process: A research design is not possible without concepts. Concepts are also central to data interpretation, and new concepts may be introduced in the latter stages of a study in order to make sense of the data.

Finally, because different disciplines and different researchers use different approaches, not all aspects of the guidelines will be applicable to all studies. For example, many researchers do not ask direct questions of respondents but instead evaluate existing sources of data: statistics, written documents (such as diaries, newspaper articles, immigration policies, and school records), and so on. In such cases comments that address the formulation of questions to respondents are obviously not applicable.

7.2 Limitations of the Guidelines

The guidelines do not always work equally well in all circumstances. In particular, they are limited when (a) relevant knowledge is insufficient; and (b) a study has no sexual relevance.

7.2.1 Limitations in Knowledge

Critiques of sexism in research are rarely possible with only superficial knowledge of a particular discipline or subject area. While we must achieve some distance from our work and from the assumptions of our own disciplines in order to detect sexism, we also need an understanding of a field of study before we can make a thorough critique of it. In doing the research for this book, for example, I was occasionally forced to eliminate an article from consideration because I lacked sufficient knowledge to understand the problem under consideration or the methodology being employed to explore it. Similarly, in the chapter on gender insensitivity, I argued that the comparison between ever-unmarried males and ever-unmarried females for the purpose of exploring the causes of female–male salary differentials is invalid because the two groups are different in essential ways: one group consists of the "cream-of-the-crop"; the other of the "bottom-of-the-barrel." My ability to make this critique hinged on my knowledge that such a difference exists and has been demonstrated. Without this knowledge, I would have failed to perceive the sexism inherent in the study. Using the guidelines will not magically make one an expert in all areas, and the more trenchant critiques (and, one hopes, nonsexist alternatives) will have to emerge from within the various disciplinary groups. Finally, we may realize that a study is sexist only after a prolonged period of time, and sometimes even when a conscious effort has been made to eliminate sexism. Using the guidelines should speed up this process, but it will be neither an easy nor a quick route to travel.

7.2.2 Studies Without Sexual Relevance

Only very rarely did I encounter in my search for examples studies that were clearly not sex or gender related. One such example is a study exploring the west-to-east migration of the early Polynesians and their Lapita predecessors in terms of recently acquired data on equatorial westerlies (i.e., winds) and associated ocean current effects.[1] Clearly this type of study is relevant to understanding an important aspect of human behavior – large-scale migration patterns by water – but since the proferred explanations all hinge on wind and current patterns and sailing constraints that result, I found no sexually relevant statements. The author once used the term "fishermen" instead of an appropriate nonsexist term,[2] but this is not a significant concept in the article. In fact, if the word had simply been dropped, nothing would have been substantially changed.[3]

One cannot properly say that the guidelines do not work in this case: they work in demonstrating that the study is not sexist. However, in most instances I would not phrase this conclusion so strongly. Returning again to the use of the ever-unmarried males and females as comparison groups, it is possible to argue in retrospect that sexism existed even though it was not immediately apparent.

7.2.3 Applicability of the Guidelines to Individual Studies versus Fields of Study

The guidelines are meant to be used primarily to assess individual research studies. The guidelines should also be helpful in conducting overview assessments of broader fields of study, although I have not yet tried to use them systematically for this purpose. Moreover, because the accumulated knowledge of different disciplines and fields of study emerges through individual studies, a critical assessment of both our own and other people's (largely unconscious) sexism is ultimately the most effective way in which to overcome sexism in research more generally.

7.3 How to Use the Guidelines

The remainder of this chapter is organized by component of the research process: formulation of the title (section 7.4), use of language (section 7.5), development of concepts (section 7.6), choice of research instrument (section 7.7), methodology (section 7.8), data interpretation (section 7.9), and policy evaluations and recommendations (section 7.10). The various ways in which sexism occurs at each stage of the research process are discussed in each section. Following the general description of the problem, each section includes a series of questions that should be asked in order to determine whether or not a sexist problem exists. The questions are meant to be used sequentially: once you have determined that a particular problem does not exist (or if you have identified a problem and remedied it), go on to the next series of questions. Each section then concludes with suggested solutions for eliminating sexism.

The checklist included in the Appendix to this book is to be used in conjunction with this chapter. It is organized along two axes. The horizontal axis identifies each stage of the research process (formulation of the title, use of language, and so on). The vertical axis is organized by type of sexist problem (overgeneralization, androcentricity, and so on). The checklist is cross-referenced to appropriate sections in the remainder of this chapter (under Text References: Identification/Resolution) and to relevant discussion in earlier chapters (under Text References: Description/Examples).

Suppose, for example, that you want to determine whether or not you have introduced sexism by your use of language. Go first to the section in the checklist labeled "Research Component: Language." Five ways in which the use of language introduces sexism are identified (note that certain types of bias, for example, double standards, can manifest themselves in several ways). In order to evaluate your choice of language, turn to section 7.4 (Sexism in Language) and ask yourself the questions listed there. If you answer "yes" to any of these questions, read through and apply the appropriate solutions. If you are unsure as to whether or not you have introduced a certain problem (or if you do not understand the problem or solutions), turn back to the appropriate section in one of the earlier chapters for a more detailed explanation.

It is worth noting, finally, that the solutions offered here are helpful only in the case of studies still in progress. For studies that have already been completed, the questions can serve to help identify sexism and thus they will alert you to problems that may exist in a relevant literature. It is hoped that this will enable you and others to avoid repeating past errors, which is, after all, what research is all about.

It may well be that there are forms of sexism that have not been discussed here. We may be blind to particular forms of sexism that reveal themselves only after we have made progress in eliminating other, more salient manifestations. I have no doubt, however, that systematically applying these questions to research in the social sciences will take us one large step forward toward a more accurate – and more useful – analysis of social reality.

7.4 Sexism in Titles

Titles are important in identifying research. They are incorporated into computer referencing systems, and are often the primary means of establishing the relevancy of someone's work to your own. They also serve as a screening mechanism that structures access to publications. Making titles appropriately reflect the content of a study will not solve all problems of sexism in research, but it will help make sexism visible. Imagine what might happen if some of the studies discussed earlier were entitled: "A Model of Male Political Participation," "Conceptions of the Male Elderly Sick Role," "Effects of Ability Grouping on Male Israeli Students," "Male Class Tells," "A Study of Male-Dominated Reform Movements in the Nineteenth Century in America," or "Men's Propensity for Warfare: An Androcentric Socio-biological Perspective." A quick computer scan, for instance, would enable the student to conclude that much research needs to be done on women.

QUESTIONS. In order to determine if a title is sexist, ask yourself the following three questions:

- Does this title evoke the image of general applicability? If yes, is it in fact equally applicable to both sexes?

- Does this title contain a sexist concept? (See section 7.6 as to what questions to address to concepts.)

- Does this title contain sexist language? (See section 7.4 as to what questions to address to language.)

SOLUTIONS. If you answered "yes" to any of these questions, either the title or the content needs to be changed.

7.5 Sexism in Language

Language may be sexist through overgeneralizing or overspecifying, through being androcentric, or through using a double standard. Using sexist language is like trying to paint a delicate picture with a large painter's brush: The tool is not sensitive enough for detailed and complicated work that needs a more precise instrument. Just as the use of a brush that is too broad and unwieldy is likely to lead to sloppy pictures, so the use of sexist language is likely to lead to sloppy thinking. While fixing the language will sometimes solve a problem, at other times it simply makes another problem visible, as happens when one makes a title content-specific, thus revealing the narrowness of the study.

Sexism in language may take several forms. The most commented-upon form of sexism in language concerns the use of male terms for generic purposes. This practice once took the form of a grammatical rule and is still regarded in this light by some people, even though it results in nonspecific language. The reverse of this form of sexism occurs when authors use generic terms when, in fact, they are dealing with only one sex, such as when they write about parents but mean only mothers, refer to workers but have only male workers in mind, and so on.

Another form of sexism in language occurs when males and females are referred to by nonparallel terms in parallel situations, such as in the expression "a man and his wife" ("he" is used as the reference point, "she" is defined in relation to him). The legal practice of wives taking their husbands' last names upon marriage is simply the same practice elevated to a legal custom.

A rather minor form of sexism in language, not comparable in importance with the others but nevertheless irritating, occurs when one sex is consistently named before the other, and when such sequencing takes on the characteristics of a grammatical rule.[4]

A fifth and very important sexist language practice concerns the use of different grammatical modes for the sexes. This issue hovers at the border between language and concepts, because it relates to data interpretation rather than simply to different modes of expression. It may not be possible to turn a written passage in which men are dealt with in the active mode (they do, act, and so on) and women in the passive mode (something is being done to them) into nonsexist form by simply changing grammatical structure. Indeed, there are instances in which one mode is clearly inappropriate (as in descriptions of the Indian custom of *suttee*, in which the active mode – widows immolating themselves – is inappropriate).

QUESTIONS. In order to determine whether or not language is sexist, ask yourself the following five questions:

- Are any male (or female) terms used for generic purposes?
- Are any generic terms employed when, in fact, the author(s) is (are) speaking about only one sex?
- Are females and males in parallel situations described by nonparallel terms?
- When both sexes are mentioned together in particular phrases, does one sex consistently precede the other?
- Are the two sexes consistently discussed in different grammatical modes?

SOLUTIONS. If you answered "yes" to any of these questions, you have identified a case of sexism in language. The remedy, if dealing with your own text, is fairly straightforward:

- In the case of the use of *sex-specific terms for generic purposes* or of *generic terms for sex-specific purposes*, use generic terms when making generic statements, and sex-specific terms when discussing one sex only.

- If males and females in *parallel situations* are referred to in nonparallel ways, equalize their treatment; for example, a "man and his wife" become a "couple," a "husband and wife," or a "woman and a man." If a wife has legally taken her husband's name, you must, of course, refer to her by her legal name, but use the same form for both males and females (for example, refer to both by their first and last names). The one exception to this rule applies when research describes a practice from a time in which nonparallel terms were or are in fact employed to refer to women and men. In such instances, you should distinguish between description and interpretation: In the case of description, nonparallel treatments must be faithfully reproduced, but in the case of interpretation, you can and should employ parallel terms.

- In cases in which *one sex is consistently named first*, alternate the sequencing in some manner.

- If the sexes are consistently discussed in *different grammatical modes*, ask yourself what is missing from the overall picture. It seems a safe enough assumption that no human being is restricted only to passively enduring or actively doing. Then, reconstruct and include the missing part. Depending on the circumstances, this may range from a very minor to a very major job.

7.6 Sexist Concepts

When we deal with concepts, we go beyond language to the meaning attached to a word or phrase *within a given context*. The same concept (for example, head of household) may or may not be sexist depending on whether it accurately describes or distorts a given social relationship. Therefore, we cannot evaluate a concept's sexist connotations without taking its context into consideration.

Concepts are a major research tool. It is sometimes difficult to see the tool itself as a potential problem. In order to recognize sexist concepts, at least two steps are necessary. First, identify concepts crucial to the study at hand. Second, subject these concepts to the questions that follow. If you answer "yes" to any of these questions, you have identified a sexist concept. Concepts may be androcentric, overgeneral, or based on a double standard or the notion of sex appropriateness. Each case is addressed separately below.

7.6.1 Androcentric (Gynocentric) Concepts

Concepts may be androcentric (or gynocentric) in any of two ways: by having a male (or female) referent, or by being demeaning to women (or men).

7.6.1.1 Construction of Ego as Male

In instances in which a concept is used as if it were generally applicable to both sexes, ask yourself who or what the concept refers to in order to determine whether or not the concept has a one-sex referent. For example, to whom does the concept of "the suburb as a bedroom community" refer? It presents itself as general but in fact refers only to a portion of the population. Similarly, the concepts of "group cohesion" and "intergroup warfare" sound inclusive but may be used with all-male referents, in which case they are androcentric.

Sometimes the referent is not hidden but is open, as in the concepts of "polygyny" or "polyandry." These are concepts that indicate a relationship that affects both sexes, but they are defined from the perspective of one sex only.

QUESTIONS. In order to determine whether or not a concept is androcentric (gynocentric), ask yourself the following questions:

- To whom or what does the concept appear to refer (who is the theoretical referent)? To whom or what does the concept *empirically* refer? Does it seem to refer to both sexes but empirically refer to one sex only?

- Does the concept refer to a relational quality expressed from the viewpoint of one sex only?

SOLUTIONS. If your answers to these questions indicate a mismatch between theoretical and empirical referents, the two must be made to match, either by changing the concept and making it sex-specific, or by changing the content and making it applicable to both sexes. Where relational qualities are concerned, they must express the viewpoint of both sexes. This may involve utilizing either a conceptual pair or a superordinate concept, whichever is appropriate.

7.6.1.2 Misogynist (Misandrist) Concepts

Some concepts demean one sex or the other, as in the case of the "masochistic woman." (Note that critical concepts that describe a negative reality are not included under this heading.)

QUESTION. In order to determine whether or not a concept is misogynistic (or misandristic), ask yourself the following question;

- Does the concept demean one sex?

SOLUTION. If you answered "yes" to this question, replace the demeaning concept with a nondemeaning one.

7.6.2 Overgeneral Concepts

In order to recognize an overgeneral concept, you need to identify both the purported referent and the empirical referent. Examples of overgeneral concepts include the use of the term "universal suffrage" to mean adult male suffrage, or the terms "childlessness" or "fertility" to describe female childlessness or fertility. Similarly, a concept is overspecific if its purported referent is one sex but it in fact applies to both sexes, as in the use of the phrase "mother tongue" to indicate the language spoken in a home in which a child grows up.

QUESTION. In order to determine whether or not a concept is overgeneral/overspecific, ask yourself the following question:

- Does the concept use a sex-specific descriptor in instances in which it is empirically applicable to both sexes?

SOLUTION. If you answered "yes" to this question, the empirical and theoretical referents must be made to match.

7.6.3 Concepts Premised on a Double Standard

There are at least three different ways in which a concept may be informed by a double standard: by being premised on unequal treatment of the sexes, by being asymmetrical, and by being value-laden within a sexual context.

7.6.3.1 Concepts Premised on Unequal Treatment of Equal Attributes in the Two Sexes

In order to recognize this double standard, you must determine whether the concept is based on an attribute that is potentially present in both sexes but is treated differently on the basis of sex. An example of such differential treatment is the use of the terms "head of household" or "head of family" to refer to adult married males, while adult married females are referred to as "spouses." The same attribute (being married) is treated differentially (the husband is designated "head," while the wife is designated "spouse").

QUESTION. In order to determine whether or not a concept is based on unequal treatment of equal attributes, ask yourself the following question:

- Is the concept premised on an attribute that is present in both sexes but is operationally defined in such a manner that it will categorize females and males differently?

SOLUTION. If you answered "yes" to this question, you need to create a concept that categorizes females and males equally if they display equal attributes.

7.6.3.2 *Asymmetrical Concepts*

In order to recognize an asymmetrical concept, you need to determine whether a sex-specific concept describes a situation, trait, or behavior that is theoretically present in both sexes but is linked to one sex only. Examples of asymmetric concepts include the use of the phrase "schizophrenogenic mother" when it is not coupled with the concept of "schizophrenogenic father," "unwed mother" when not linked with "unwed father," and "maternal deprivation" when not linked with "paternal deprivation."

QUESTION. In order to determine whether or not a concept is asymmetrical, ask yourself the following question:

- Does the concept refer, in a sex-linked manner, to a situation, trait, or behavior that exists for both sexes?

SOLUTION. If you answered "yes" to this question, change the concept so that it expresses *human* attributes in sex-nonspecific terms.

7.6.3.3 *Value-Laden Concepts*

A value-laden conceptual pair is one in which a sex-related division is created by assigning different labels that contain value judgments about certain characteristics when no such value judgments are warranted. (There are cases in which such value judgments are warranted, as when dealing with violence or abuse). Examples of value-laden conceptual pairs include "field independence" and "field dependence," "productive work" and "unproductive work," and "primary earner" and "secondary earner."

QUESTIONS: In order to determine whether or not a concept is inappropriately value laden (i.e., sexist), ask yourself the following questions:

- Does the conceptual pair correspond largely to a sexual division?
- If so, is the differential value attached through choice of words to the male- and female-dominated attributes justified?

SOLUTION. If you answered "yes" to the first question and "no" to the second, reformulate the conceptual pair so that equal value is assigned to male- and female-dominated attributes.

7.6.3.4 Concepts Premised on Notions of Sex-Appropriateness

In all known societies, people consider certain behaviors and traits to be more appropriate for one sex than for the other; however, there is great variability in what is considered appropriate (or "normal" or "healthy") for either sex in different societies. Such concepts as "sex roles" and "sex identity" are useful descriptors, but when a given behavior or trait is presented as unproblematically "appropriate," it introduces a double standard.

QUESTION. In order to determine whether or not a concept is based on some notion of sex appropriateness, ask yourself the following question:

- Is the concept premised on the notion that certain *human* behaviors, traits, or attributes are appropriate for one sex only?

SOLUTION. If you answered "yes" to this question, identify socially sex-assigned attributes by descriptive but not prescriptive labels in order to eliminate the assumption of sex *appropriateness*.

7.6.4 Familistic Concepts

Concepts that attribute individual properties, attributes, or behaviors to families or households are gender insensitive. Examples of such gender-insensitive concepts include use of the term "family support systems" when it is generally individual women who render support, or use of the variable "family income" when dealing with earned income of one individual.

QUESTION. In order to determine whether or not a concept is gender insensitive, ask yourself the following question:

● Does the concept attribute individual properties, attributes, or behaviors to families or households?

SOLUTION. If you answered "yes" to this question, identify individual properties, attributes, or behaviors as such.

7.6.5 Concepts Based on Sexual Dichotomism

Sexual dichotomism occurs when concepts are derived from the notion that the sexes are two entirely discrete social as well as biological groups. This happens whenever human traits are defined as masculine or feminine, or human biological phenomena (such as testosterone or progesterone) are labeled "male" or "female."

QUESTION. In order to determine whether or not a concept is based on sexual dichotomism, ask yourself the following question.

● Does the concept define certain human attributes, capacities, traits, or behaviors as either masculine or feminine?

SOLUTION. If you answered "yes" to this question, identify human attributes or capacities as such, rather than as belonging to one sex or the other.

7.7 *Sexism in the Research Design*

Sexism may enter into the research design in the form of androcentricity, gender insensitivity (including familism), or a double standard (including sexual dichotomism). Different aspects of a research design are applicable to different kinds of studies, but at a minimum, all research designs involve choosing a research question and using some frame of reference.

7.7.1 *Sexism in the Choice of Research Question or Frame of Reference*

Sexism can enter into the research design in two ways: through the relevant literature and through the design of a particular study. Because so much social science research has, by and large, been sexist, chances are that the way in which a particular topic is customarily addressed in the relevant literature will be sexist as well. It is therefore necessary to assess *critically* the relevant literature with respect to potential sexist elements, in order to avoid making the same mistakes. This applies to all components of previous research, including language used, concepts employed, and so on, but is particularly important for the overall frame of reference. There are three ways in which sexism may enter into the choice of research question or adoption of a framework: The framework adopted may be androcentric, the major research question chosen may be formulated in an androcentric or gyno-centric manner, or the research question may be based on a double standard.

7.7.1.1 Androcentric Frame of Reference

An androcentric frame of reference is created when the major research question is formulated in such a way that only men are seen as actors while women are treated as objects that are acted upon.

This is the case, for example, with the sociobiological explanation of "intergroup warfare" in "primitive man" discussed previously. In such instances, women become largely invisible. Similarly, an androcentric framework is adopted when male behavior is treated as the norm and female behavior is seen only in relation to this norm, as was the case in another article we discussed that explained the "choice" of reasons for divorce by female and male petitioners. Finally, a frame of reference is androcentric when it results in attaching blame to women where it is unjustified (as when blaming victims, rather than the perpetrators, for sexual assaults, or blaming mothers for problems with children without considering the role of fathers or extraneous factors).

QUESTION. In order to determine whether or not a research frame of reference is androcentric, ask the following question:

- Substitute the word "woman," or such nonsexist terms as "person," "individual," "worker," "citizen," "consumer," "patient," or "elderly person," each time the author uses the so-called generic term "man." Does the statement still make sense?

SOLUTION. If these substitutions render the statements nonsensical, you have uncovered an androcentric bias. In order to remedy this problem, recast the study by exploring the females' situation, or revamp the study as one pertaining to one sex only. This latter alternative is not appropriate when the topic deals with relational issues (for example, "group cohesion" where there are both women and men in the group).

QUESTION.

- Are men treated as actors, women as acted upon?

SOLUTION. If you answered "yes," add a second set of questions about women as actors and men as acted upon to the research design.

QUESTION.

- Is male behavior taken as the norm, and female behavior as the deviation that needs to be explained?

SOLUTION. If you answered "yes," either expand the framework by assessing male behavior against female behavior, or establish a genuinely sex-unrelated behavior as the norm. The latter is not feasible if the behavior in question is strongly sex differentiated.

QUESTIONS.

- Are women blamed? If so, is the blame justified?
- Are women victims or perpetrators?
- Are the perpetrators held responsible for their deeds?
- Is the role of male participants in the process adequately considered?
- Are overall structural factors adequately taken into account?

SOLUTION. Where there are victims, perpetrators must be held responsible for their actions. Consider the role of male participants in the process as carefully as that of female participants; take overall structural factors into account.

7.7.1.2 *Androcentric or Gynocentric Formulation of Research Questions*

An androcentric or embryonically gynocentric[5] formulation of the research question exists when a phenomenon that affects both sexes is studied primarily by focusing on one sex only. This is often the case with social stratification studies, in which women have been largely excluded from consideration, or in family studies, in which men have been largely excluded from consideration in their role as parents.

QUESTIONS. In order to determine whether or not a research question is androcentric (gynocentric), ask yourself the following questions:

• Does the phenomenon under consideration affect both sexes?

• If so, does the literature give adequate attention to the role of both sexes? In particular, in studies concerning families and reproduction, has the role of men been given adequate attention? In all other subject areas, has the role of women been given adequate attention?

SOLUTION. If a phenomenon affects both sexes but has been studied primarily with respect to one sex only, include the excluded sex in your research design. Alternatively, this may be a case in which a one-sex study is appropriate, provided that it focuses on the hitherto excluded sex. When a field of study is so biased toward one sex that the other sex is virtually ignored, the problem may lie with the overall *balance* of the research rather than with any one individual study.

7.7.1.3 *Research Questions Based on a Double Standard or Sex Appropriateness*

In two-sex studies, respondents are sometimes asked different questions even though the same instrument may be used on both sexes. This is often the case with studies using some measure of socioeconomic status, or when both women and men are asked about a potential work–family conflict for married women, but not for married men.

QUESTION. In order to determine whether or not a research question is based on a double standard or sex appropriateness, ask yourself the following question:

- Are both sexes asked the same questions?

SOLUTION. If not, develop instruments that ask the same questions of both sexes.

7.7.2 Choice of Research Instruments

Sexism may also enter the research design through the choice of research instruments that are based on either a double standard or sexual dichotomism.

7.7.2.1 Double Standards in Choice of Research Instruments

Researchers occasionally develop different instruments for male and female subjects. This may even be done in response to an androcentric instrument in order to overcome such bias, as is the case with an instrument especially developed to measure the socioeconomic status of women. However, data generated from such instruments do not allow us to make comparative statements. In a few exceptional cases, different instruments for the two sexes are necessary, as when examining certain physical illnesses and sex-related symptoms. However, even in such cases the questions should be as nearly equivalent as possible.

QUESTIONS. In order to determine whether or not a research

instrument introduces a double standard, ask yourself the following questions:

- Is the same instrument used for both females and males? If not, is the use of a differential instrument justified by physical differences between the sexes?

SOLUTION. If different instruments are used without compelling reasons, develop an instrument that is applicable to both sexes. If different instruments are necessary, justify them in detail.

7.7.2.2 Sexual Dichotomism in Choice of Research Instruments

Particular research instruments occasionally divide the sexes into two discrete groups, even though in reality females and males overlap in some of the dichotomized characteristics. This is the case with masculinity–femininity scales. The use of such instruments results in empirical reality being subordinated to stereotypic notions.

QUESTION. In order to determine whether a research instrument introduces sexual dichotomism, ask yourself the following question:

- Does the research instrument divide the sexes into two discrete groups when, in fact, they have overlapping characteristics?

SOLUTION. If you answered "yes," adopt new research instruments that do not dichotomize overlapping distributions of traits.

7.7.3 Androcentric Choice of Variables

In two-sex studies, androcentricity may enter the research design through the designation of "important" variables. For example, in the studies on group cohesion among early hominids, the research emphasizes male-dominated activities without considering female-dominated activities (such as nursing, cooking, and care of children) that may very well contribute to or affect group cohesion.

QUESTIONS. In order to determine whether or not the choice of variables has introduced an androcentric bias, ask yourself the following questions:

- What are the major variables examined in this study? Are these variables equally relevant to women and men? If most of the variables pertain to men, is there an equivalent number of variables pertaining primarily to women?

SOLUTION. If you answered "no," correct the imbalance by including variables that affect women. In areas in which we know little about the major factors that affect women, a pilot study may be required.

7.7.4 Neglecting the Sex of Participants in the Research

Gender insensitivity occurs when the sex of participants in the research process is neglected. In studies in which both sexes participate as subjects but the breakdown by sex is not reported, crucial information necessary to interpret the findings is missing. Likewise, the sex of research personnel who come into direct contact with respondents may affect the respondents' answers. Finally, the authorship of statements is important in understanding possible biases, omissions, and emphases.

QUESTIONS. In order to determine whether gender insensitivity has been introduced by failing to report the sex of participants in the research process, ask yourself the following questions:

- Who are the relevant participants in the research process?
- Is their sex reported?
- Is their sex controlled for? If not, is the potential effect of the sex of the participants explicitly acknowledged and discussed?

SOLUTION. Always report the sex of participants. Control for the sex of participants wherever possible. If this is impossible for practical reasons, acknowledge and discuss the potential effects of the sex of the various participants in the research process.

7.7.5 Taking the Family as the Smallest Unit of Analysis

Taking the family as the smallest unit of analysis is not necessarily sexist. A researcher who wishes to describe the various types of families within a society will properly take the different types of families or households as the smallest unit of analysis. It is sexist practice (familism) only in two instances: (1) if the family is attributed behaviors, experiences, benefits, problems, or detrimental effects that are, in fact, attributes of individuals within the family unit (as is the case when individual income is treated as "family" income, or when the family is treated as a care support system for the elderly when only individuals within the family render such care); and (2) when the family is credited with experiencing something (whether positive or negative) in instances in which the same event may have disparate effects on the various family members (as in the cases of the effects of marriage or divorce, joint utility functions, or the assumption of the optimization of family resources).

QUESTIONS. In order to determine whether or not the family has properly been taken as the smallest unit of analysis, ask yourself the following questions:

- Is the issue under consideration anything that is in fact an attribute, experience, or behavior of an individual within the family unit rather than of the unit as the whole?

- Is it possible that the event under consideration may have different effects on various family members?

SOLUTION. If you answered "yes" to either of these questions, the use of the family as the smallest unit of analysis is inappropriate. Identify the individual actors within the unit as such, and study the potentially different effects of the event under investigation by the sex of family members. This may require a drastic revision of the research design.

7.7.6 Inappropriate Comparison Groups

Much gender-sensitive research requires comparing male and female groups with each other. However, male and female groups are occasionally compared when it is inappropriate for the comparison at hand (although not necessarily for other purposes). For instance, if the incomes of male and female groups are to be compared, it is important to ensure that the groups are otherwise comparable (on variables known to influence income, such as education, type of occupation, and so on). The failure to use appropriate comparison groups may lead either to the false attribution of a phenomenon to sex when it is in fact due to some other variable, or to the false attribution of a phenomenon to some other factor when sex is in fact the important variable.

QUESTIONS. In order to determine whether or not gender insensitivity has been introduced by using inappropriate comparison groups, ask yourself the following questions:

- Are any explicit or implicit comparisons made between the sexes? If so, are the sex groups being compared equivalent on all those variables that are likely to have an influence on the outcome under investigation?

SOLUTION. If you answered "no" to the second question, create comparable groups. If this is impossible for practical reasons (for example, you cannot meaningfully compare social factors leading to breast cancer in women and men), carefully list and discuss the variables that differentiate the two groups.

7.8 Sexism in Methods

Obviously, a short book of this type cannot discuss all of the methods used in the social sciences. Some issues that might have been discussed in this section were discussed in the previous section on research design because the distinction made here between research design and methods is an artificial one. Choice of methods is an integral part of the overall research design as are concepts and language used.

So far, we have not identified any method that could not be used in either a sexist or nonsexist manner. In principle, then, methods per se are neither sexist nor nonsexist; it is the way in which they are used (or misused) that makes them (non)sexist.

Methods may be sexist in several ways: (1) through the use of instruments in a manner based on sexual dichotomism; (2) if they formulate questions in an androcentric manner; (3) if they rely on notions of sex appropriateness as an explanatory variable; (4) if they treat other-sex opinions as statements of fact about the other sex; or (5) if they incorporate a double standard.

7.8.1 Androcentricity in the Validation of Research Instruments

Androcentricity is introduced in methods if a research instrument is developed and validated on males only but is subsequently used on both sexes (if it were developed and validated on females only and were subsequently used on males and females, it would be an instance of gynocentricity).

QUESTIONS. In order to determine whether or not androcentricity (gynocentricity) has been introduced through the validation of research instruments, ask yourself the following questions:

* Has this research instrument been developed and validated on one sex only? If so, is it used on both sexes?

SOLUTION. If you answered "yes" to both questions, restrict the use of the instrument to the sex for which it was developed and validated; alternatively, redevelop and validate the instrument with both sexes.

7.8.2 *Gender Insensitivity in Reporting on Sample*

Researchers occasionally fail to report the sex composition of their sample, as was the case in a number of articles considered in Chapters 3 and 4. Failure to report the sex composition of the sample makes adequate assessment of the meaning of the data impossible.

QUESTION. In order to determine whether or not gender insensitivity has been introduced in this manner, ask yourself the following question:

* Is the sex composition of the sample adequately reported?

SOLUTION. If you answered "no," report the sex composition of the sample.

7.8.3 *Sexist Bias in the Formulation of Questions*
or Questionnaires

Individual questions or questionnaires may be biased because they use sexist language, are formulated in an androcentric manner, or are based on some notion of sex appropriateness. Questions employ sexist language if they use "man" in its supposedly generic sense (as in the earlier example of a study exploring attitudes toward "a *man* who admits he is a communist" in order to measure tolerance). Questions that do not allow for the total range of possible answers because males are taken as the norm and females are judged accordingly are androcentric (for example, as in asking respondents to agree or disagree with the statement "It is generally better to have a man at the head of a department composed of both men and women employees" and omitting "It is generally better to have a woman ..."). Finally, questions may be biased by being premised on the notion of sex appropriateness (for instance, by assuming a particular division of labor between the sexes as normative when asking "How often do you feel a conflict between being a mother and working?" without asking an equivalent question about fathers).

QUESTIONS. In order to determine whether or not a questionnaire or an individual question is biased in a sexist manner, ask yourself the following questions:

- Does the question use generic terms for sex-specific purposes or sex-specific terms for generic purposes?

- Does the question take one sex as the norm for the other, thus restricting the range of possible answers?

- Is the question premised on some notion that particular behaviors are appropriate for one sex but not for the other, either explicitly or implicitly, by failing to ask equivalent questions for the other sex?

SOLUTIONS. If sexist language is employed, change it to nonsexist language. If one sex is taken as the norm, reformulate the question to allow for the complete range of theoretically possible responses. If the question assumes that a particular behavior is appropriate for one sex only, reformulate the question to probe the existence of this behavior in both sexes.

7.8.4 Sexual Dichotomism in Methods

Sexual dichotomism is introduced by any method that divides *human* attributes into male and female attributes (as is the case in masculinity–femininity scales) or which treats the sexes as categorically different groups on the basis of *human* attributes.

QUESTION. In order to determine whether or not sexual dichotomism has been introduced in methods, ask yourself the following question:

- Does this particular method categorize males and females into discrete groups on the basis of attributes that can be found in *both* groups?

SOLUTION. Categorize nondiscrete traits in nondiscrete ways.

7.8.5 Treating Other-Sex Opinions as Facts

Researchers sometimes ask members of one sex about the other sex. This may provide very useful information, so long as the researcher keeps in mind that the opinions of one sex about the other must never be confused either with fact or with the opinions of the other sex about itself. Where such confusion occurs, we are dealing with an instance of gender insensitivity.

QUESTIONS. In order to determine whether or not gender insensitivity has been introduced in this manner, ask yourself the following questions:

- Are opinions asked of one sex about the other (including in indirect form, for example, by using historical information)? If so, are they treated as opinions of one sex about the other or as fact?

SOLUTION. If you answered "yes" to these questions, reinterpret other-sex opinions as statements of opinions and no more.

7.8.6 Double Standards in Coding Procedures

If the same responses are interpreted differently by sex (by using different coding instructions, for example) a very blatant double standard is created.

QUESTION. In order to determine whether or not coding procedures are based on a double standard, ask yourself the following question:

- Are identical coding procedures used for females and males?

SOLUTION. If you answered "no," make coding procedures uniform for both sexes.

7.9 Sexism in Data Interpretation

Many of the sexist problems that arise in data interpretation are a consequence of sexism introduced earlier in the research process: in concepts, in the research design, in methods. By eliminating sexism in these components, some of the sexism in data interpretation will also be eliminated. Nevertheless, it is possible for sexism to enter independently at the data interpretation stage through androcentricity, overgeneralization, gender insensitivity, or sex appropriateness.

7.9.1 Androcentricity in Data Interpretation

Data may be interpreted in an androcentric manner by using a male viewpoint or frame of reference, by accepting or justifying female subjugation or male dominance, or by blaming victims.

It is difficult to disentangle the use of a male viewpoint or frame of reference in the research design from that in the data interpretation. Once data are gathered from such a male perspective, it will be difficult or even impossible to avoid carrying this problem over into the data interpretation stage. However, in cases in which there is no way to alter existing data collection processes (for example, in the case of secondary analyses), at a minimum, any existing bias in the research design must be pointed out, and appropriate caution must be exercised in interpreting such data.

The justification of female subjugation or male dominance in the name of some supposedly superior value (for example, cultural tradition or the integrity of ethnic customs) is a direct abrogation of the human rights of females. The defense of bodily mutilation or death or abrogation of basic human rights through data interpretation or otherwise is always inappropriate. Similarly, it is equally inappropriate to blame a clear victim (as in the case of father–daughter incest); interpreting data to blame the victim only adds insult to injury.

QUESTIONS. In order to determine whether or not an androcentric bias has been introduced during data interpretation, ask yourself the following questions:

- Are the implications of findings for both females and males explicitly considered?

- Are biases in the data collection process explicitly acknowledged and their implications discussed?

- Is there any justification of female subjugation or male dominance? Is any form of bodily mutilation, death, or other abrogation of human rights justified in the name of a supposedly higher value?

- Is there a clear victim? If so, is the victim blamed for her (occasionally his) victimization?

SOLUTIONS. If you answered "yes" to the first question, consider the implications of findings for both sexes. If you answered "yes" to the second question, acknowledge any biases that cannot be eliminated, explicitly discuss the importance of such bias, and adjust your conclusions accordingly. If you answered "yes" to the third set of questions, describe and analyze your findings but in no case excuse or justify them. If you answered "yes" to the final set of questions, identify the circumstances (or individuals) that led to victim-blaming and eliminate such blame from your interpretations.

7.9.2 Overgeneralization in Data Interpretation

Overgeneralization in data interpretation occurs when researchers use only a one-sex sample or focus their attention on one sex only but phrase their conclusions in general rather than in sex-specific terms.

QUESTIONS. In order to determine whether or not data interpretation is overgeneral, ask yourself the following questions:

- Is only one sex considered? If so, are conclusions drawn in general terms?

SOLUTIONS. If you answered "yes" to both questions, make the conclusions sex-specific, or, alternatively, alter the research design so that both sexes are considered.

7.9.3 Gender Insensitivity in Data Interpretation

Gender insensitivity in data interpretation takes two basic forms: ignoring sex as a socially significant variable, and ignoring a relevant sex-differentiated social context. As an example of the first form, researchers occasionally collect data on both sexes but fail to analyze these data by sex. This problem may occur during the research design (for example, by utilizing a computer program that does not allow for analysis by sex), or it may be restricted to the interpretation stage if the researcher simply fails to look at the importance of sex. Such oversight may result in serious distortions in conclusions, particularly in cases in which the distribution of traits is systematically different for the sexes. Results based on such gender-insensitive data interpretation will give an inaccurate picture for both males and females.

Decontextualization is the second way in which data interpretation can be gender insensitive. This occurs when researchers fail to realize that the same event or situation (for example, marriage, divorce, political participation, and so on) may have very different implications for the sexes.

QUESTIONS. In order to determine whether or not data interpretation is gender insensitive, ask yourself the following questions:

- Are data collected on both sexes? If so, are they analyzed by sex? Is the difference or lack thereof between the sexes considered?
- Does the particular situation or event under consideration have potentially different implications for the two sexes? Have these been explicitly considered and discussed?

SOLUTIONS. If you answered "yes/no/no" to the first set of questions, reanalyze the data by sex and discuss the results. If you answered "yes/no" to the second set of questions, explore and discuss the potentially different implications of the impact of such events or situations on both sexes.

7.9.4 Sex Appropriateness in Data Interpretation

A double standard is introduced in data interpretation when data are interpreted as being consistent with some preconceived notion about what is (or is not) appropriate for one sex or the other.

QUESTION. In order to determine whether or not a double standard based on sex appropriateness has been introduced during data interpretation, ask yourself the following question:

- Are sex roles (or sex identities) seen as normatively appropriate?

SOLUTION. If you answered "yes" to this question, acknowledge sex roles (and sex identities) as socially important and historically grown, but make clear the fact that they are not necessary, natural, or normatively desirable.

7.10 Sexism in Policy Evaluations and Recommendations

Policy studies are one particular type of social science study and are singled out here for consideration because of their effect on people's lives: some policy studies actually do lead to policies, or at least influence them to some degree. It is, of course, impossible to make nonsexist policy evaluations or recommendations if the preceding research has been sexist because the requisite knowledge base is not present. On the other hand, it is quite possible to make sexist policy evaluations or recommendations on the basis of nonsexist research; policies are necessarily informed by some value against which they are gauged, whether this is done explicitly or implicitly. Given this, the nature of policy recommendations and evaluations thus depends on whether both the research and the values on which it is based are informed by the notion of sex equality or inequality.

For instance, let us assume a study conducted in a nonsexist manner concludes that a particular economic policy would disproportionately hurt employed wives. If policymakers hold that the right to work under equivalent circumstances should apply equally to women and men, they will recommend rejecting such a policy. If they hold that "male breadwinners" should be favored over "secondary earners," they will evaluate the policy positively. There are several ways in which policy evaluations and recommendations can be sexist.

7.10.1 *Gender Insensitivity in Policy Evaluations and Recommendations*

It is possible that the same policy may have different effects on women and men because of the historically grown differences between the sexes. In order to assess whether or not this will be the case, it is necessary to conduct studies in a gender-sensitive manner, separately assessing the impact of policies on women and men. Particular care must be taken to ensure that the family is not treated as a unit in which individual family members share uniform experiences or benefit (or suffer) equally from particular policies.

QUESTIONS. In order to determine whether or not a policy evaluation or recommendation is gender insensitive, ask yourself the following questions:

- Does this policy affect both sexes?
- If yes, is the position of the sexes comparable with respect to the important factors that inform and are governed by this policy?
- Is the effect of this policy positive for both sexes?

SOLUTIONS. If you answered "yes" to all of these questions, the policy is not gender insensitive, but you should clearly demonstrate, not simply affirm, that this is the case. If you answered "yes" to the first question but "no" to any of the others, the policy is biased, but this does not necessarily mean that it should be abandoned. If the policy is meant to right an old unfair situation, for example, there may be good reason for maintaining it. Or if the policy is disadvantageous for one sex but is nevertheless highly desirable for other reasons, it may be more appropriate to develop compensatory policies. (Such a situation might apply if environmental concerns supported reducing work opportunities within one sector.) In any case, arguments supporting such policies should be made explicit; state the values that underlie such policies and demonstrate how the policy supports them. If there is no such justification for a biased policy, or if compensatory policies cannot be enacted, the policy should be reevaluated in terms of its impact on both sexes.

7.10.2 Double Standards in Policy Evaluations and Recommendations

Analysts occasionally recommend policies that reward or punish people differentially by sex for the same trait. Such is the case when mothers involved in custodial disputes are penalized for having a paying job while fathers are rewarded for it, or when "surrogate" mothers are subjected to highly intrusive investigative measures while even mildly intrusive measures are considered unacceptable for the social fathers and their spouses.

The issue is more complex when such differential treatment is based on some other, ostensibly nonsexual, criterion that corresponds largely to a division by sex. This is the case, for example, when primary earners are treated differently from secondary earners with respect to entitlement to public benefits.

QUESTIONS. In order to determine whether or not policy evaluations or recommendations are based on a double standard, ask yourself the following questions:

- Are the same circumstances evaluated differently on the basis of sex?
- Is there a division that corresponds largely to a division by sex and for which differential treatment is recommended?

SOLUTION. If you answered "yes" to these questions, the policy should be reevaluated so that the sexes are treated in the same manner, regardless of whether such differential treatment is directly or indirectly based on sex.

Notes

1 Ben R. Finney, "Anomalous westerlies, El Nino, and the colonization of Polynesia," *American Anthropologist* 87, 1 (1985): 9–26.
2 Ibid., p. 21.
3 The sentence as a whole reads: "While I doubt if many successful colonies were planted by fishermen or coastal voyagers accidentally blown to some uninhabited island, a scenario that solely stresses systematic voyages of exploration and colonization presumes far too much order and predictability in what must have been a most uneven and hazardous expansion."
4 I once had my usage of "women and men" in a manuscript reversed to "men and women" by a copyeditor. Upon my protest she told me that this was a grammatical rule. I let it go because there were more important issues to fight about, but it is clearly a sexist rule.
5 Gynocentricity is characterized as embryonic because at the present time it is virtually impossible to be truly gynocentric – we are missing all the necessary tools for it, due to the overwhelming androcentric bias.

Epilogue

In this book, we have looked at a number of examples of sexism in existing research and have developed a set of guidelines for recognizing sexism in existing research and avoiding it in current and future research. In the process, we have identified seven different types of sexism. It is important to realize that sexism comes in different forms: little is gained if we eliminate one type of sexism only to replace it with another one.

These guidelines for nonsexist research provide us not with substantive answers but with a new set of questions. This is how true progress in knowledge takes place: not primarily by finding new answers to old questions (although that, of course, is also important) but by posing new questions that will eventually generate new answers. Becoming aware of sexism in research does just that. It provides a perspective that allows us to ask new questions and thus opens up new ways of looking at the world. To illustrate this principle in action, let us return to a few of the examples that were used previously to illustrate certain types of sexism.

The following are questions that might be asked about four of the topics that we discussed in this book: intergroup aggression and conflict, social stratification, fertility and childlessness, and the elderly. Note how the elimination of sexist bias that ignored, distorted, or misinterpreted sex differences enables us to see these problems in a different light; new questions, new research agendas, and eventually new answers and new policies thus emerge almost automatically.

Intergroup Aggression and Conflict

- Did women participate in group conflict? In what manner?

- What effect did the introduction of extra-group women have on group cohesion? Did group cohesion exist between males and females? If not, what form did social cohesion take, and what was the relationship of mothers to their offspring? If yes, how was cohesion affected by the entry and departure of women? What was the nature of female–female relations? How did it compare to female–male relations? To male–male relations?

- What is the meaning of "inclusive fitness" for female members of a group? How does this relate to women's role in warfare?

Social Stratification

- What constitutes "human capital" for a woman? What are the effects of accumulating the capital for women? Does the same asset constitute human capital for men? If so, what are its effects on men? If not, why not? Are there gender-neutral forms of human capital?

- Since women have historically undertaken the care of the young for intrinsic rather than extrinsic rewards, are there also men who undertake comparably demanding and important tasks for intrinsic rewards? If so, who are the men, and what are the tasks? If not, why not? How does this affect our understanding of social stratification in general?

Fertility and Childlessness

- What are the fertility rates of men? How have they changed over time? In what way are they different from female fertility rates?

- What is the age-specific proportion of men who father children with women to whom they are not married? Are they single or married to someone else? Is there a group of men who father such children comparable in size to the group of unmarried women who give birth, or is it only a relatively small group of men who are responsible for a relatively large number of pregnancies?

The Elderly

- Are there gender differences in the way elderly sick women and men are perceived? If so, what are they? Do males and females have the same or different perceptions of elderly men and women? What are the policy implications of any differences that do exist?

- Do elderly women and men use different coping resources? If so, what are they? Are some resources that facilitate coping in one sex neutral or negative in their impact on the other sex? If so, why? How does this affect our understanding of the relationship between coping resources and health effects in general?

This is only a small sampling of questions that emerge from an analysis of sexism. They should, however, suffice to demonstrate the immense array of questions that present themselves once we have critically examined the existing literature for sexist problems.

It is not easy to accept the idea that well-established ways of looking at the world may be inherently flawed, as the hero of our first chapter, the Square from Flatland, found when he was bodily lifted by his guide, a Sphere, out of his two-dimensional homeland to look at it from the third dimension:

An unspeakable horror seized me. There was a darkness; then a dizzy, sickening sensation of sight that was not like seeing; I saw a Line that was no Line; Space that was not Space; I was myself and not myself. When I could find voice, I shrieked aloud in agony, "Either this is madness or it is Hell." "It is neither," calmly replied the voice of the Sphere, "it is Knowledge; it is Three Dimensions: open your eye once again and try to look steadily."

I looked, and, behold, a new world!

If, like the Square, we dare to open our eyes and look steadily at the world as it presents itself from the perspective of both sexes, we will find a new richness in what we thought were familiar and well-charted grounds. Introducing the perspective of women into a previously androcentric frame of reference opens up infinite research possibilities. Looking at men as gendered beings – and not as humanity pure and simple – makes us understand them differently and more realistically. By embracing the principles and practices of nonsexist research, we too can behold a new world.

Appendix: Nonsexist Research Checklist

Type of Problem	Description of Problem	Text References: Description/Examples	Text References: Identification/ Resolution
	Research Component:Title		
Overgeneralization	Title generalizes content of study when in fact research has been carried out on only one sex	3.3, 3.6	7.4
Based on sexist concept	Title reflects and/or contains a sexist concept (see below)	3.2.2, 3.3	7.4
Based on sexist language	Title contains sexist language (see below)	3.2	7.4
	Research Component:Language		
Overgeneralization	Sex-specific terms used for generic purposes	3.2.1	7.5
Overspecificity	Generic terms used for sex-specific purposes	3.2.2	7.5
Double Standard	Nonparallel terms used for females and males	5.2.1	7.5
Androcentricity	One sex consistently named first	2.3.1	7.5
Double Standard	One sex consistently discussed in the passive mode, the other in the active mode	5.2.2	7.5
	Research Component:Concepts		
Androcentricity	Ego constructed as male in concepts that are presented as general	2.2.2, 2.3.2	7.6.1.1

Term	Description		
Androcentricity	Concept expresses relational quality from the perspective of one sex only	2.2.2, 2.2.5, 2.3.2	7.6.1.1
Androcentricity	Concept demeans women	2.3.2	7.6.1.2
Overspecificity	Concept defined as sex-specific when it is applicable to both sexes	3.4	7.6.2
Double Standard	Concept classifies the same attribute differently on the basis of sex	5.3.1	7.6.3.1
Double Standard	Concept identifies a behavior, trait, or attribute with only one sex when in fact it is or may be present in both sexes	5.3.2	7.6.3.2
Double Standard	Concept or conceptual pair ascribes a different value to traits more commonly associated with one sex	5.3.3	7.6.3.3
Sex Appropriateness	Concept based on the notion of "sex-appropriate" behavior, traits or attributes	6.2	7.6.3.4
Familism	Concept attributes individual properties to families of households	6.3.3	7.6.4
Sexual Dichotomism	Concept attributes human capacities to one sex only	6.4.2	7.6.5

Research Component: Research Design

Frame of Reference

Term	Description		
Androcentricity	Study designed from a male perspective	2.2.1, 2.3.3	7.7.1.1
Androcentricity	Female behavior assessed against male behavior, which is taken as the norm	2.2.4	7.7.1.1

Choice of Research Question

Term	Description		
Androcentricity	Women excluded from research design even when the research question affects both sexes	2.2.3	7.7.1.2

Type of Problem	Description of Problem	Text References: Description/Examples	Text References: Identification/Resolution
Gynocentricity	Men excluded from research design, especially in areas concerning family and reproductive issues	2.3.3, 5.4.1	7.7.1.2
Double Standard/ Sex Appropriateness	Both sexes included in research design but different research questions asked about females and males	5.4.1, 6.2.1	7.7.1.3
Choice of Research Instrument			
Double Standard	Different research instruments used for the two sexes	5.4.2	7.7.2.1
Sexual Dichotomism	Research instrument divides males and females into discrete groups and assigns human attributes to each of them	6.4.3	7.7.2.2
Variables Examined			
Androcentricity	Variables related to women's specific situation in two-sex studies not adequately taken into account	2.3.3	7.7.3
Sex of Participants in the Research Process			
Gender Insensitivity	Study does not take into account the fact that female and male subjects may react differently to comparable situations	4.5	7.7.4

Gender Insensitivity	Study does not take into account the fact that male and female researchers and research staff may elicit different responses from human subjects	4.5	7.7.4
Gender Insensitivity	Study does not take into account the fact that data obtained from informants and authors of statements (whether written, oral, audiovisual, or other) are likely to vary by sex	4.5	7.7.4
Unit of Analysis			
Familism	The family used inappropriately as smallest unit of analysis	6.3.2, 6.3.3	7.7.5
Comparison Groups			
Gender Insensitivity	Noncomparable groups of females and males used	4.6	7.7.7

Research Component: Methods

Research Instrument Validation			
Androcentricity	Research instrument validated for one sex only but used for both sexes	2.3.4	7.8.1
Sample Composition			
Overspecificity/ Gender Insensitivity	Researcher fails to report on sample composition by sex	3.5.2, 4.2	7.8.2
Questions and Questionnaires			
Overgeneralization	Questions use sexist language	3.5.1	7.8.3

174

Type of Problem	Description of Problem	Text References: Description/Examples	Text References: Identification/Resolution
Sample Composition			
Androcentricity	Questions do not allow for total range of possible answers for both sexes	2.3.5	7.8.3
Sex Appropriateness	Questions premised on notion of sex-(in)appropriate behavior, traits, or attributes	6.2.1	7.8.3
Choice of Research Instruments			
Sexual Dichotomism	Research instrument stresses sex differences with the effect of minimizing the existence and importance of sex similarities	6.4.4	7.8.4
Other-Sex Opinions			
Gender Insensitivity	People (including experts) asked about behaviors, traits, or attributes of members of the other sex, and such information treated as fact rather than opinion	4.4	7.8.5
Coding Procedures			
Double Standard	Identical responses coded differently by sex	5.4.3	7.8.6
Research Component: Data Interpretation			
Androcentricity	Findings interpreted within male frame of reference	2.2.5	7.9.1
Androcentricity	Forms of female subjugation, abuse, or restriction seen as trivial	2.2.4	7.9.1

Androcentricity	Forms of female subjugation, abuse, or restriction seen as normal or defended in terms of cultural or ethnic tradition	2.2.4, 2.2.6	7.9.1
Androcentricity	Victim rather than perpetrator made responsible for the crime	2.2.5	7.9.1
Overgeneralization	General conclusions drawn from an all-male (or all-female) sample	3.6	7.9.2
Gender Insensitivity	Data collected (or available) for both sexes but not analyzed by sex	4.3	7.9.3
Gender Insensitivity	Interpretation of sex similarities or differences fails to take the different social positions of the sexes into account	4.6	7.9.3
Sex Appropriateness	Sex-specific roles accepted as normal and desirable	6.2.2, 6.2.3	7.9.4

Research Component: Policy Evaluations and Recommendations

Gender Insensitivity	Failure to take into account the fact that policies have different impact on the sexes due to the historically grown differences in the position of the sexes	4.3, 4.7	7.10.2
Double Standard/ Sex Appropriateness	Same circumstances evaluated differently on the basis of sex	5.6.1, 6.2.2	7.10.2
Double Standard	Differential treatment by sex hidden behind ostensibly nonsexual distinction	5.6.2	7.10.2

Index

About the Author

Margrit Eichler is Professor of Sociology at the Ontario Institute for Studies in Education. She has written and lectured widely on the subject of nonsexist research and is the author of several books, including: *The Double Standard: A Feminist Critique of Feminist Social Science* (1980) and *Canadian Families Today: Recent Changes and Their Policy Consequences* (1983). Professor Eichler received her Ph.D. from Duke University in 1972 and has served in various capacities as an advisor to the Canadian government on the status of women.